Reading Habermas

For
my mother
and in memory of
my father

Reading Habermas

David M. Rasmussen

With a bibliography by
René Görtzen

Basil Blackwell

Copyright © David M. Rasmussen 1990

First published 1990

Basil Blackwell, Inc.
3 Cambridge Center
Cambridge, Massachusetts 02142, USA

Basil Blackwell Ltd
108 Cowley Road, Oxford, OX4 1JF, UK

Library of Congress Cataloging in Publication Data
Rasmussen, David M.
    Reading Habermas/David M. Rasmussen; with a bibliography by
René Görtzen.
        p.   cm.
    ISBN 0−631−15273−3 − ISBN 0−631−15274−1 (pbk.)
    1. Habermas, Jürgen.   I. Title.
B3258.H324R37   1990
193−dc20

British Library Cataloguing in Publication Data
A CIP catalogue record for this book is available from the British Library.

Typeset in 10 on 12 pt Ehrhardt
by Setrite Typesetter Limited, Hong Kong
Printed in Great Britain by Billing & Sons Ltd., Worcester

Contents

Acknowledgments

There are those to be thanked: first and foremost, Jürgen Habermas for his friendship, openness, graciousness and general good humor demonstrated during our many discussions on the three extended occasions I spent as his guest in Munich in 1982, and in Frankfurt in 1986 and 1988. He does indeed personify the communicative ideals for which his work has become known. At the same time, although his work is the subject, I take full responsibility for the contents of this book.

I am grateful to the many readers of the manuscript, in full or in part, for their valuable suggestions. Axel Honneth, Hauke Brunkhorst, Klaus Günther, Günther Frankenberg, Steven White, Richard Bernstein and Jacques Taminiaux were most helpful in this regard. I should like to thank the various colleagues, friends and students who made critical suggestions regarding various chapters of the book as presented in lecture form. In particular colleagues at the Italian Phenomenological Society at Milan, the Scottish Phenomenological Society at Dundee, the philosophy departments at the University of Essex, the University of St Andrews, the University of Aberdeen, the University of Louvain, the State University of New York at Stony Brook, the Center for European Studies at Harvard University, and at the Institute for Social Science of the Technical University of Munich became partners in the intense dialogue whose outcome is recorded on these pages.

I thank administrators and colleagues at the various granting agencies which made extended study in Germany possible. The Mellon Foundation (1980−1), The Fulbright Commission (1981−2 and 1988), and Boston College Fellowships (1986 and 1987−8) enabled me to complete the project which became the subject of this book.

I should also like to thank Heide Natkin for her kind assistance and hospitality in Frankfurt, Deanne Harper for her, as usual, expert assistance with the manuscript, and Tracey Stark for her superb work on the final stages.

I have had the good fortune to have excellent editors. Special thanks go to René Olivieri who convinced me to write this book and to Stephan Chambers whose considerable editorial skills are witnessed in this text. In the end we became collaborators.

To my good friends in Maine, Carl Weymouth and Eleanor and Ardell Chadbourne, who were encouraging in their enthusiasm for the project and respectful of my need for solitude, I owe special thanks.

I am especially indebted to René Görtzen for choosing this occasion to publish his excellent bibliography of Jürgen Habermas's work.

Special thanks are owed to Mary Vogel whose unexpected appearance during the final stages of this project were a source of constant encouragement and delight.

Cambridge, Massachusetts
December 31, 1989

1

The Dilemmas of Modernity

My own preoccupation with the thought and work of Jürgen Habermas began in the early seventies when, after having worked and written in the areas of hermeneutics and the phenomenology of language, I turned, as did many of my generation, to a consideration of German nineteenth-century post-enlightenment thought, with a particular emphasis on Hegel and Marx. It was in that context that I began to read, and occasionally to write on, the works of Jürgen Habermas.

In retrospect, it appears that I was not immediately persuaded. During that period I wrote a vaguely disguised critique of Habermas's interpretation of Marx, defending Marx on instrumental reason against Habermas's attack.[1] At that point I claimed that Marx was not guilty as charged, for succumbing to the seducements of positivism. At about the same time, I wrote a review essay on *Legitimation Crisis* which attacked Habermas in a rather nasty way for having usurped and used the traditions of Weber and Marx for his own purposes.[2] Habermas kept on writing. Indeed, it has been something of an effort just to keep up with the prodigious output of publications which continues to appear.

For my part, I have been slowly persuaded. I am persuaded, that is, that the direction Habermas's thought has taken in recent years has been fruitful and worthy of the most careful and serious attention of those interested in, as it turns out, not only the developments of social and political philosophy, but also the developments of law, ethics and even literary theory. In a review essay on what must be said to be his most extraordinary effort to date, the two volumes of *The Theory of Communicative Action*, I suggested that it was to the eighties what John Rawls's *A Theory of Justice* was to the seventies, a monumental work which would require the serious reflection of the decade.[3] As it turned out, that pre-

[1] David M. Rasmussen, "Marx: On Labor, Praxis and Instrumental Reason," *Dialectics and Humanism*, 3, (1979), pp. 37–52.

[2] David M. Rasmussen, "Legitimation Crisis: Late Capitalism and Social Theory," *Cultural Hermeneutics* 3–4, (1976), pp. 59–70.

[3] David M. Rasmussen, "Communicative Action and Philosophy: Reflections on Habermas's *Theorie des Kommunikativen Handlens*," *Philosophy and Social Criticism*, 9:1 (Spring, 1982), pp. 2–28.

diction was neither inaccurate nor difficult to make considering the range and depth of the work.

To be sure, the book represents a break; not a rupture in the Althusserian sense, but a distancing from and a reconsideration of themes represented in earlier writings. Traces of the old themes are there — the preoccupation with Marx, the fascination with the transition from ancient to modern politics, the attempt to overcome positivism, the desire to adapt social theory to the conditions of modernity, the struggle to deal with mentors and predecessors in the so-called Frankfurt School. But new themes are also present: the desire to develop a systematic approach to modernity, the paradigm shift to the philosophy of language, the problematic of rationality and rationalization, the establishment of an approach which would enable later forays into discourse ethics, literary theory and the critique of post-modernism; even, one might suggest, the bases for the more recent essays on politics and the German debate over recent history are to be found in Habermas's book. Along with a few of its successors, *The Theory of Communicative Action*, has engendered a rather large secondary literature.

Perhaps one of the ironies of all this is that Habermas is no longer considered the exclusive property of the left, but is, to his own surprise and chagrin, almost mainstream. And, certainly to no one's surprise, introductions to his work abound. My own reaction to this rather extraordinary output has been one of, to quote Machiavelli from another context, both amazement and satisfaction.[4] The former pertains to the sheer brilliance of the attempt to take most of the preoccupations of social philosophy and place them in a completely new context. The latter reaction reflects the delight in the enterprise itself, namely, to have, as it were, kept the faith. Thanks to treatises like those referred to above, we can still talk about a just society, radical democracy, an open society, in short, that idea which Hegel thought was the principle of historical development itself, i.e., freedom.

Unfortunately, or perhaps fortunately, there are questions: has Habermas succumbed to the very temptations of those whom he so ruthlessly critic- ized for giving up their youthful passions for the sedate scientism of older age?[5] Is this enterprise, which apologists are so eager to claim as foun- dationless, still based on the practices of old-time epistemology?[6] Does this

---

[4] Nicholo Machiavelli, *The Prince* (New York, Mentor, 1952), p. 55.

[5] There is a rather large body of criticism centering on precisely this point, with which I will deal in detail later. The argument is that Habermas has so attempted to legitimate his theoretical claims scientifically, a practice which some find dubious at best, that he either confuses aspects of his political program with science or he abandons solidarity with the oppressed in the name of science. See chapter 3.

[6] I regard Richard Rorty's "Kantian grid" argument, although made before the publication

enterprise, which claims to grant to all the rights of communication, in its very universalism succumb to the insidious infection of sexism?[7] Is the road to communication simply the masking of an underlying passageway to power?[8] Indeed, the criticism is legion. In an essay on Habermas and the fate of modernity,[9] I suggested that the harbor had been mined and the test would be to find out if this ship could make it to the open sea. To be sure, as captain, Habermas has done a masterful job of not only keeping his vessel afloat, but also of staying on course. He has indeed stimulated criticism, invited it, responded to it, in an often heated and lively fashion.

Certainly, one does not begin such an analysis *de novo*, independent of that growing body of critical literature that surrounds *The Theory of Communicative Action*, but in the center. If I were to paint the picture with the boldest brush strokes possible, I would suggest that there is a certain tension in Habermas's thought between the paradigm shift from the philosophy of consciousness to the philosophy of language and its commitment to modernity. In one sense, the so-called new, post-1981 program endorsed and advanced by Habermas is very traditional. Older epistemological distinctions still abound. The crucial distinction between the scientific, the ethical or moral, and the aesthetic is still there, under another name to be sure, but there just the same.[10] Equally, basic evolutionary or progressivist claims, both ontogenetic and philogenetic, are retained, but within the confines of a philosophy of language. The categories of normativity so dear to Kant and the German enlightenment are still there, but now under the rubric of discourse. The claim for the primacy of communication over other modalities of linguistic interaction is said to be read out of the scientific character of language or discourse and not as a statement of the

of *The Theory of Communicative Action*, to be the most challenging in this regard. *Philosophy and the Mirror of Nature*. (Princeton, NJ, Princeton University Press, 1979), pp. 379–89.

[7] Carol Gilligan makes this argument indirectly by criticizing Lawrence Kohlberg's theory of the stages of moral development, upon which Habermas relies for his theory of ontogenetic development. Others have attempted to develop arguments in this regard. See Nancy Frazer. "What's Critical About Critical Theory? The Case of Habermas and Gender," *New German Critique*, 35 (Spring/Summer, 1985), pp. 97–131.

[8] This is the post-structuralist critique of Habermas. Axel Honneth, although not a post-structuralist, has made an excellent argument in this regard. See *Kritique der Macht* (Frankfurt am Main, Suhrkamp, 1985).

[9] David M. Rasmussen, "Habermas and the Fate of Modernity," *Theory, Culture and Society*, 2:3 (1985) pp. 133–144.

[10] I am aware that the scheme has changed from the one Habermas proposed in *Knowledge and Human Interests* to the one presented in *The Theory of Communicative Action*. While the former referred to the manner in which knowledge could be divided, the latter refers to the way in which experience, as understood through modalities of communication, can be divided. The issue is whether Habermas has rid himself of all traces of epistemologically derived distinctions, as he has claimed.

way things should be. What may not be immediately apparent in the Habermasian program, but is none the less the case, is that there is a certain kind of agenda that seems to be endorsed, i.e., egalitarianism, universal rights, radical democracy, support of new social movements, etc., presented under the rubric of reconstructive science, the claims of which are read out of a philosophy of language.

Indeed, we discover that with some modification the very program for philosophy which characterized post-enlightenment German thought, the project of modernity, finds its endorsement within the confines of a theory of communicative action. On the surface, or so it would appear, there is really nothing wrong with that. But, at a deeper level, questions arise. Inasmuch as the theory of communication finds its origin in a theory of the nature of linguistic usage, the burden to be borne by this particular orientation towards language will be precisely the project of modernity. And yet, can the project of modernity be formulated through the theory of communication, which in turn is based on a philosophy of language?[11] Indeed, the skeptic might argue that the philosophy of language and the project of modernity have nothing to do with each another. The evidence for such a claim would be that the project of modernity was formulated precisely within the confines of the philosophy of consciousness with its concern for the development of a subject, while the philosophy of language, in its contemporary form at least, begins with the repudiation of that very subject. Taken further, the scenario might read, the project of modernity and the philosophy of language have essentially two different agendas, one justifying subject-centered reason, the other finding whatever reason there is within the confines of linguistic usage. Can the dilemmas of modernity be reformulated under the rubrics of a philosophy of language which is centered on a theory of communication? That is the question which is at the core of the post-1981 Habermasian reflection. Quite simply, can the two agendas be brought together? Of course, Habermas believes that they can. Indeed, that is the wager: to defend what he once called old European human dignity[12] in the new and reconstructed context of his version of the philosophy of language.

One might clarify the peculiar tension alluded to above. The task is not to endorse the project of modernity as such. On this rare occasion Habermas would agree with Nietzsche: the classical formulation as such was doomed. Rather, his task is to rehabilitate the project of modernity by reconstructing it vis-à-vis the theory of communication, i.e., communicative action, communicative reason. Hence, the task is to overcome the pessimism of late

---

[11] The question is whether communication, in principle, is emancipatory.

[12] Jürgen Habermas, *Legitimation Crisis* (Boston, Beacon Press, 1975), pp. 142–3.

modernity, the indulgence of his predecessors, by resolving the dilemmas of subject-centered reason in the new paradigm of communicative action. Characteristically, here Habermas is able to don his two most favored hats, that of the careful, technical diagnostician, and that of the great speculative thinker. In his most recent thought, the dilemma of modernity is most carefully attended to in the most programmatic of manners. In *The Theory of Communicative Action* the diagnosis begins with Weber, in *The Philosophical Discourse of Modernity* it begins with Hegel; yet whether given Hegel's positive or Weber's negative readings of modernity, the result is the same: the failure of subject-centered reason.

The story, as it is narrated in the context of these two works, is a dramatic one. Reason, imprisoned in the modern subject, could only express itself instrumentally, resulting in the transition from a positive reading of the powers and capacities of reason in the modern world (Hegel) to a negative one (Weber). In this scenario, Weber and Nietzsche become allies. The twentieth-century result culminated in *Dialectic of Enlightenment*, which, in principle, agreed with Weber's dire prediction that liberation through reason is as negative as it is positive.[13] In the latter case, knowledge brings about further repression. But this, Habermas has attempted to show, was a false diagnosis. Here one must make the distinction between subject-centered reason and reason itself. Indeed, subject-centered reason is victimized by its own instrumental formulation, but not reason itself, or reason in its other form, namely communicative reason. At its base level, the assumption is that the project of modernity can be redeemed. Weber's diagnosis is in principle false; and not only Weber's, but also those of Horkheimer, Adorno, Nietzsche, Heidegger, Foucault, and Derrida. One begins to see that the Habermasian enterprise rests upon a rather massive claim which, if successful, can undermine much of contemporary philosophy.

Among German philosophers these days it is rather fashionable to read the history of philosophy in terms of the philosophy of language. Tugendhat, Apel and others have attempted to unmask the problems of particular thinkers in the history of philosophy as essentially problems of the philosophy of consciousness, which can be diagnosed and resolved by the philosophy of language. Habermas, in his attempt to redeem the project of modernity for his own purposes, has drawn heavily from this endeavor while, at the same time, placing his own peculiar stamp upon it. The program of early critical theory was to conceive of the development of

---

[13] Max Horkheimer and Theodor Adorno, *Dialectic of Enlightenment* (New York, Social Studies Association, Inc. 1944. German reissue S. Fischer-Verlag GmbH, Frankfurt am Main, 1969).

modern thought in the context of the growth of instrumental reason. Horkheimer's distinction between traditional and critical theory represented an attempt to free reflection from this association. Hence, the task of critical theory was one of emancipation from instrumental reason.

Habermas, in his earlier work, endorsed this program, making it more comprehensive and systematic while at the same time directing the project of critical theory towards the comprehensive critique of positivism. By endorsing the paradigm shift to the philosophy of language according to the fashion in contemporary German thought, he has been able to incorporate the retainable elements of the previous program of critical theory within the larger paradigm of the philosophy of language. The result of this "synthesis" is that the philosophy of language, under the rubric of communication, is employed to do essentially what the earlier program, i.e., critical theory, attempted but could not accomplish given certain strictures within the philosophy of consciousness. The project of modernity is but the other side of the program of early critical theory. Through the transition to the philosophy of language they can be both criticized and redeemed, that is, according to this particular reading of the potentialities and capacities of the philosophy of language. My point is that this is a very *particular* reading of the powers and capacities of the philosophy of language.[14]

I am not claiming, at this point, that this is either a false or improper reading *per se*. However, it is a reading shared by few, even on the German front. And this is what I mean by the tension between the program of the philosophy of language on the one hand, and the project of modernity on the other. Seldom, in other receptions of the philosophy of language, has such a use or interpretation been made. Instead, the transition to the philosophy of language has meant a departure from the above-mentioned project. Habermas, however, makes his case more distinctive. He claims that embedded within the linguistic paradigm, under the rubric of communication, one finds the fundamental assertions of the project of modernity in their reconstructed form, as essentially scientific claims. One finds the very structure of communicative discourse to be emancipatory, to embody the claims of a reconstructed project of modernity; an insight, to be derived from the nature of language as such.

Of course, our skeptic, whom we left a moment ago, would want to know if the emancipatory insight is really derived from the nature of language as such, or if it could be that this was one of those normative or utopian claims coming from the "passion" of its author.[15] One might reflect for a

---

[14] Only if a very esoteric variety of the philosophy of language is acceptable can this project work. This is not to pre-judge the particular reading as false. However, in pointing to the distinctiveness of this reading, I will highlight it as precisely that which either makes or fails to make the Habermasian project possible.

[15] Here the debate concerns the role and legitimacy of reconstructive science.

moment with the skeptic about the meaning of this assertion. If the project of modernity could be separated from the claims of the paradigm shift to the philosophy of language under the rubric of communication, would it mean that the whole enterprise would falter? If so, what would be the measure of its failure? Obviously, a position which claims to be systematic must itself submit to systematic criteria. Perhaps the overall project of the theory of communicative action would be redeemable, but on grounds other than those originally given.[16]

What has made the Habermasian project so appealing for so many, and I include myself here, is that he has found a way of legitimating the project of human emancipation in a world where appeal to the philosophy of language represented something less than passionate commitment. He has also attempted to anticipate the dangers and pitfalls involved in the construction of a synthesis between the two endeavors. Much of the criticism generated by this rather bold attempt has fallen precisely here. Either he has erred on the side of science or on the side of passion.[17] In the case of the former, he has, so the critics seem to suggest, robbed social and political thought of its human and passionate content. This would be the emancipation of critical theory itself resting now, through the Herculean efforts of its most recent proponent, above human struggle on the secure foundations of science. In the case of the latter, passion, those defending the scientific claims of language would want to know what kind of science this is that finds the drive toward emancipation at the very roots of language. At best, this is scientific reconstruction with a passionate intent. At worst, this is a kind of mixture of the claims of analytic philosophy in which all insights have been stirred into a kind of potpourri where recognition is lost.

There is no doubt that the project of modernity[18] is a subject that, in one form or another, runs throughout Habermas's mature work, both early and late. The problem is, quite simply, how to redeem it. The argument has, over the years, become more nuanced, more comprehensive, and, one

---

[16] The systematic claim that Habermas has made throughout his later work is that he has freed his overall project from reliance upon epistemology and foundationalism — the preoccupations of the so-called philosophers of the subject.

[17] Habermas has attempted to make his emancipatory claims scientific and not utopian. The two kinds of criticism that arise from this attempt are naturally those which would emphasize either the scientific or the utopian at the expense of the other. I will deal with them in detail later.

[18] This is a claim which requires some justification on my part. The term, "the project of modernity," is derived from one of Habermas's more recent works, *The Philosophical Discourse of Modernity*, tr. Frederick Lawrence (Cambridge, MA, The MIT Press, 1987), p. 131. I take this to be a summation of earlier attempts to find ways of legitimating the enlightenment project of emancipation, an enterprise which has dominated the works of Habermas for at least the last two decades.

might even state, more interesting. Habermas, complex and difficult though
he is as a writer, has always had a flair for the dramatic. One recalls the
opening scene of *Knowledge and Human Interests* where we are invited to
imagine the great debate of the modern period as one in which everyone is
asking a single question: how is reliable knowledge possible?[19] A more
recent dramatic image is that of a discourse − a discourse on modernity.
Imagine! As if some of the great philosophical thinkers of the nineteenth
and twentieth centuries − Hegel, Marx, Nietzsche, Heidegger, Horkheimer,
Adorno, Bataille, Foucault and Derrida − were all engaged intentionally in
a discourse on modernity. As a metaphor for the Habermasian program,
somehow, it must be admitted, the image works. It illustrates the dilemma
to which the theory of communicative action will address itself.

That dilemma, as we discover, is not a new one. It began with Hegel,
whose consciousness of the *Zeitgeist* led him to understand the dilemma of
"modernity", namely, that philosophy would have to develop normativity
out of itself.[20] I take this small and seemingly innocent task to be both
paradigm and paradox of Habermas's work, providing the starting point for
both the dialectic of enlightenment and the discourse on modernity. Again
and again in this discourse we shall see attempts to engage the dialectic of
enlightenment, and again and again we shall see how thought twists around
itself in such a way that normativity is anything except something generated
out of itself; always, rather, something to fall back upon, always something
dredged up from a previous age, from an earlier time.

The discourse on modernity begins from the striking realization that
precisely the "modern" problematic is that reason has no recourse other
than itself, has no tradition to fall back upon, no myth to rely upon, no
religion for which it may exist as a rational counterpart. Philosophy suddenly
finds itself alone, perhaps even at an end. Hence, the discourse on modernity is one which will test the very limits of reason, will define its
parameters; a discourse which will, in the name of reason, at least originally,
attempt to avoid its dialectical subversion.

In the end, the discourse on modernity becomes a solemn affair in which
the partners in the dialogue become silent. One by one they turn away, or
attempt to, from the "modern" problematic to abandon the dialectic of
enlightenment by going behind it to absolve the tensions of modernity in a
Western archaism, where the word "foundation" would change to "historical origin" and "enlightenment" would be replaced by the "nobility" of
the past. Habermas argues that this celebrated "turning" is an illusion

---

[19] Jürgen Habermas, *Knowledge and Human Interests*, J. J. Shapiro. (Boston, Beacon Press,
1971), p. 3.
[20] Ibid., p. 10.

indulged in by those who, in their very attempt to escape the dilemmas of modernity, bear all its traces.

The mark of a great systematic thinker is to make it appear that the solution for which the thought is generated is a necessary one. To do that, it is essential that the problem to which that thought is addressed is unavoidable. The project of modernity appears on the scene as a kind of double paradox. To engage it results in the peculiar seduction of the dialectic of enlightenment, namely, to be trapped by it, as was Hegel, as was Marx, as were Horkheimer and Adorno. To attempt an escape represents a kind of nihilistic leap into a primordial past brought on by the very attempt to be avant-garde, leaving the present, as it were, unexamined. Nietzsche, the fearless leader, led Heidegger, Bataille, Foucault and Derrida out of modernity, but for reasons that could only be conceived in the terms given by the very project of modernity. The lesson to be learned is twofold: one *must* engage the problematic of modernity; a cursory glance at theoretical history tells us there is no escape. However, and this is the rub, all attempts to engage the project of modernity have ended in failure.

Habermas, as he has attempted to deal with the project of modernity over the years, always returns to Hegel to state the problem: Hegel, the first to write his philosophy out of the dilemma of modernity. Hegel, the first to wreck upon the shoals of modernity. How could philosophy regenerate itself in a modernity that had abolished tradition? That is the question from which not only Hegel's thought is said to evolve, but from which it can be said modern thought evolves. This is no simple or unbiased look at Hegel. As usual, one is looking for the rational paradigm which appears momentarily, only to vanish with subsequent preoccupations. Hegel, after an early and very brief infatuation with art as having the power of reconciliation, turns to other areas. According to this interpretation, it is the power of reconciling reason, manifest in some form of communicative action which Hegel almost discovers and which, subsequently, in his preoccupation with the philosophy of the subject, he abandons.[21] The problem with the philosophy of the subject is that it is not truly intersubjective, conceiving of the relationship of individuality to universality in terms of the interactions of a self-consciousness. As such, self-consciousness will eventually link up with absolute knowledge which leads simply to an endorsement of that which is. In other words, the attempt to embody the emancipatory principle of enlightenment in the philosophy of the subject ends by legitimating all forms of institutional repression. This is the paradox of the dialectic of enlightenment.

[21] Compare this strategy with an earlier one, i.e., Habermas's "Labor and Interaction: Remarks on Hegel's Jena *Philosophy of Mind*." in *Theory and Practice* (Boston, Beacon Press, 1973), pp. 142–69.

To be sure, that kind of critique, as Habermas well knows, was first voiced by the most renowned of the Hegelians of the left, Karl Marx, even though Marx was unaware of the dilemmas of the philosophy of the subject as well as the significance of the option which Hegel is said to have rejected. What is important about this reading is its endorsement of Hegel's relatively rapid rejection of art as the foundation of reconciling reason, and his turn toward a political solution to the problem of modernity. Obviously, among the solutions to the problems of ethical life that Hegel could have attempted was that of radical democracy.[22] As is well known, he rejected it. Why he rejected that option is open to speculation. There is a technical explanation as well as an ideological one. Technically, he may have been unable to carry through the full implications of a truly intersubjective form of rationality, even though, God knows, he tried. Limited to the schema of a philosophy of the subject, he could only conceive the reconciliation of universality and individuality in the context of a self-consciousness. Ideologically, and I use the term loosely, merely to indicate a set of ideas, Hegel may not have been ready for radical democracy; at least one may surmise that he became less ready for it as time went on. For whatever of these reasons, Hegel resisted a "communicative" solution. Theoretically, one could agree with Habermas, it could have been an option. But what is significant for us is that Habermas chooses the Hegelian approach to the problem of modernity even though on the finer points of theory he differentiates himself from Hegel. The obvious test of his thought will be whether Habermas can outwit the self-declared paradox implicit in the dialectic of enlightenment.

It is also important to note that Habermas sanctions Hegel's "political" orientation to the problem of modernity, while rejecting an "aesthetic" solution. As is well known, Hegel was the first to attempt to reconcile the various differentiated spheres[23] which were peculiar to the experience of modernity. Hegel, using the newly developed discipline of political economy, was able to see early on that the imperatives of civil society, which were distinctive, must be reconciled with those of the state, a form of social existence pre-dating modernity. Reason finds its own ground by working through these spheres, mediating them, reconciling them one with another. However, in Habermas's view, it does it "too well."[24] Reason falls back upon absolute knowledge and loses the "genuine self-understanding of modernity." Hegel's orientation is political in the sense that he turns to political life, ancient and modern, to find the form of reason manifest in the

---

[22] Clearly, the communicative paradigm is based on the idea of radical democracy.

[23] Interestingly enough, this is where Hegel and Weber are one in their recognition of modernity as the dilemma of a differentiated rationality.

[24] Ibid., p. 63.

political institutions of the day. Hegel's early fascination with *Volksgeist* as the embodiment of reason illustrates that. His solution, however, was radically institutional, justifying the complete subordination of the individual will to the institutional orders of the day. Clearly, according to Habermas, he made the wrong choice. "A different model for the mediation of the universal and the individual is provided by the *higher-level intersubjectivity of an uncoerced formation of will* within a communication community existing under constraints toward cooperation."[25] In other words, Hegel rejected radical democracy as the repository of reason. Here Habermas establishes the basis for an interesting challenge. If he (Habermas) is to outwit the dialectic of enlightenment by making the switch from the philosophy of the subject to the philosophy of language, the philosophy of language chosen will have to sustain the dynamics of a political solution to the problem while at the same time developing a normativity which arises out of itself. Our skeptic will want to know precisely how this political solution can be rendered scientific, i.e., how can this normativity be developed out of claims other than those derived either from utopian considerations or, in any case, brought into modernity from the outside?

One can see that, as the discourse on modernity develops, an expanding set of conditions has to be met in order that the practice of philosophy might continue. The plot thickens. In this scenario, three historic groups meet to take up the challenge left by Hegel: the Hegelians of the left, the Hegelians of the right, and Nietzsche and his followers. Significantly, the first two take up the political solution endorsed by Hegel, revising it in accord with their own aims. The third turns toward the aesthetic solution, opting out of the paradox of modernity altogether, or at least attempting to do so. Here, of course, the stage is set for our modernity. While the problematic of the Hegelians of the left leads us to the dilemmas of liberal and leftist thought today, the solution opted for by the Hegelians of the right emerges as contemporary neo-conservatism. The option endorsed by Nietzsche and his followers leads directly to post-structuralism. While one leftist solution, *praxis* philosophy,[26] retains the illusions of the paradigm of production with its positivist overtones, the paradigm originally endorsed by Marx, the Hegelians of the right entertain the illusion that they can roll back cultural modernity while endorsing social modernity. They sustain both Hegel's uneasy feelings about the advance of the bourgeois and his desire to reinstate the forces of religion in a secular world. In this analysis, both the left and the right engage the dialectic of enlightenment only to

---

[25] Ibid., p. 60.

[26] Among others, Agnes Heller has been particularly sensitive to this criticism. For her position, particularly on the question of normativity and modernity, see, *Beyond Justice*, (Oxford, Cambridge, MA, Basil Blackwell, 1987).

succumb to its enigmas. In the case of the former, *praxis* philosophy, the paradigm of production is said to be contingent upon that of communication, while in the case of the latter, there is no reaching back behind the enlightenment, as it were, to establish normativity from pre-enlightenment resources. Hence, if we were to read the contemporary scene correctly, it is as if the left and the right were destined to follow in the fated footsteps of their forebearers. In so doing, they succumb to the seductive powers of the dialectic of enlightenment.

Regarding the Hegelians of the left and those of the right, Habermas is on very familiar territory. Both engage the issues of reason and rationality, enlightenment and dialectic — the dilemma of the appropriate political solution to modernity. Not so with Nietzsche. Nietzsche is different. By comparison with the Hegelians, Nietzsche is arrogant. Somehow, Nietzsche represents the paradox of modernity while undermining it, rejecting it, and, along with it, the theoretical history of reason, rationality, rationalization, development, progress, and evolution. Nietzsche somehow endorses the radicality of aesthetic modernity as it was first perceived in Kant, while at the same time returning to the origins of the West. Nietzsche, the philologist, finds the alternative to enlightenment in the archaism of the West. Where Hegel found *Volksgeist* in the Greeks, Nietzsche somehow went behind Hegel to find an experience more original in the experience of art. Nietzsche's is the aesthetic experience somehow to be contrasted with the political as that which has primacy.[27]

Nietzsche outwits the enlightenment, or does he? That is the ambiguous question which raises the dilemma of enlightenment all over again. But this

---

[27] It seems that there are two strains of thought about modernity coming out of the German enlightenment and post-enlightenment periods, one deriving from Hegel and the other originating with Kant. What I will show is that Habermas clearly opts for the Hegelian as opposed to the Kantian side, specifically in terms of his reading of modernity. Hegel, as I point out in the above text, clearly chooses the political solution. He, of course, had read and absorbed Aristotle. The *polis* includes everything. Hegel, as a consequence, subordinates the aesthetic to the political. Habermas follows Hegel in this regard. The aesthetic is one of the three forms of differentiated rationality, associated with subjective expressiveness. Habermas reflects both Hegel and Aristotle in this regard, choosing to keep the aesthetic under the watchful eye of a more comprehensive form of reason. Kant was much more radical, one might say modern, in his view of the aesthetic. In the *Critique of Judgment* Kant makes it clear that the aesthetic does not conform to either science or morality, but has a rationality of its own. In the end, Kant is much more subtle than Hegel. The aesthetic could not be so easily reconciled to the other spheres. In my view, Nietzsche's thought owes a part of its origin to this Kantian insight. No doubt Habermas's desire to overcome the aesthetic will strain his interpretation of Nietzsche and his followers. Later, I will probe the issue of aesthetics again, not in defence of Nietzsche, but regarding the legitimacy of the tripartite scheme into which Habermas places modern rationality. One might question the "modernity" of this view of modernity.

time in a different way. In one sense Nietzsche takes up the orientation of Hegel's earliest writing, *Die Älteste Systemprogram*, which proclaimed myth and art as the regenerative form for modern reason. That was romanticism. And romanticism shared with the enlightenment the idea of emancipation. Nietzsche's endorsement of the aesthetic puts him with the avant-garde program of aesthetic modernity. But Nietzsche gives up on the idea of emancipation. Identity, individuation, uniqueness, ideas at the very heart of the program of emancipation, are abandoned in his return to the Dionysian. Nietzsche is no longer interested in the idea of truth. Beyond truth and falsity, beyond good and evil, lies taste, "the yes and the no of the palate." This is the Habermasian characterization. It appears that Nietzsche has exempted himself from the curse of enlightenment by over-coming the value spheres of scientific truth and moral validity, by undermining the Western theory of rationalization, by returning to the archaic.

Habermas's strategy has to be somehow to bring Nietzsche back into the fold, to develop arguments that show that he has not outwitted the en-lightenment. To unmask the unmasking of the theories of power, that theoretical trash heap which, from Nietzsche's point of view, contains modernity's accumulation of rational potentialities and actualities. That is no easy task. The key is the concentration on "aesthetic modernity," to be distinguished from other forms of modernity. Nietzsche only goes beyond modernity by accepting one of the two solutions to its dilemma, namely, the idea of the aesthetic regeneration of reason. Ultimately, Nietzsche, who abandons reason to the various discourses on power, retains only the sense of heightened aesthetic sensibility which was the cornerstone of the program of aesthetic modernity. In other words, the Nietzsche who abandons mo-dernity cannot quite abandon it. The leap from reason to taste entails aesthetic judgment, which in turn is based upon reason. "But he cannot legitimate the criteria of aesthetic judgment that he holds on to because he transposes aesthetic experience into the archaic, because he does not recognize as a moment of reason the critical capacity for assessing value that was sharpened through dealing with modern art − a moment that is still, at least procedurally, connected with objectifying knowledge and moral insight in the processes of providing argumentative grounds."[28]

Instead, for Nietzsche, the aesthetic form of reason becomes the "other of reason." Here, one perceives the trace of the Habermasian (Hegelian) preference for the political over the aesthetic solution. If one chooses the political solution, one can designate the aesthetic as only one of a plurality of spheres into which the experience of modernity is differentiated. Hence-forth, the aesthetic must compete with the moral and the scientific for its

[28] Jürgen Habermas, *Theory and Practice*, (Boston, Beacon Press, 1973), p. 145.

validity. It must distinguish itself from claims of truth and normativity. In this sense, the aesthetic bears that trace of rationality that links it to modernity and the rationality problematic that it engenders. Ideally, all the spheres of modern life would be linked together communicatively, yet differentiated according to meaning. Of course, Nietzsche wants to repudiate differentiation in order to return to the primordial archaic experience of undifferentiated being. Equally, Nietzsche wanted to concentrate on the aesthetic to the exclusion of the moral and the scientific. No doubt, much of the critique of post-structuralism hinges on the legitimacy of this attempt. If it is possible to return to undifferentiated being, the myth of the subject would be dissolved. If it is possible to dismiss all but aesthetic forms, the dialectic of enlightenment would be abandoned.

I have suggested, in constructing arguments against Hegelians of the left and the right, that Habermas is on familiar territory. With them, the political solution to the problem is not in question, the problem lies in the proper mediation of the spheres. With Nietzsche the case is different. Here, one must argue that the concentration on the aesthetic realm is inappropriate. But, in order to do that, it is necessary to give to the theory of aesthetics an Hegelian cast, to reduce the aesthetic to another form of rationality. Hegel did that in order to abandon it. Art reached its fullness with the Greeks only to fall into decadence in modernity. Reason, in the form of *Geist*, adopted another form, the state, in which it would manifest itself. Habermas does not repeat that error, but he does, like Hegel, force aesthetics into a rational mold. Once that is done, it is possible to see aesthetics only as a competing form of reason subject to criteria similar to that of the other forms of reason. Aesthetic judgment would then invoke procedural criteria which could distinguish aesthetic from other forms of reason. But this is true if and only if aesthetic judgment is analogous to other forms of rational apprehension.[29]

As Habermas's thought develops, one begins to realize how close the dark side of the dialectic of enlightenment is to his own thought, to his own tradition, to the thought of his mentors. Here, the battle for the proper focus of reason takes on almost psychological characteristics; the need to redeem not only the project of modernity, but also to set his mentors straight, absolving critical theory from its seduction by the Nietzschian turn. In *The Theory of Communicative Action*, Horkheimer and Adorno are accused of succumbing to the dilemmas of the philosophy of the subject. In *The Philosophical Discourse of Modernity*, Habermas returns, this time under the influence of his critique of Nietzsche, to take a second look.

---

[29] My point is that this claim works only if one makes what must be seen from the point of view of the *Critique of Judgment* as an illegitimate "aesthetic reduction."

Somehow, that late turn of critical theory doesn't fit into the neat scheme of the Hegelians of the left, the Hegelians of the right and the followers of Nietzsche, from which the discourse on modernity is said to evolve. In a curious way, *Dialectic of Enlightenment* partakes of the two major traditions: the bastard child of both Hegel and Nietzsche. The thesis of that book, which affirms the circularity of myth and enlightenment, the one reverting to and being transformed into the other, radicalizes the notion of critique to the point where it loses its rational foundation. Both philosophers view enlightenment as a two-sided process in which achieving of enlightenment results in succumbing to a new mythology. Modernity's attempt to outwit the enlightenment is achieved at the price of instrumental reason, which requires both external objectification and internal repression in a frenetic attempt to keep the myths at bay. In the end, their attempts to deal with the project of modernity, in this interpretation, result in a total obfuscation of that project.

Habermas's critique is both interesting and revealing. He tries to undermine the abject cynicism of late critical theory by reaffirming what we first found in Hegel as the political, as opposed to the aesthetic, response to the project of modernity. For his mentors, science had been absorbed by instrumental reason, while morality had been absorbed by the positivist understanding of science. Even art, corrupted by mass culture, had been "emptied of all critical and utopian content." In this view, the three great moments of reason "regress to rationality in the service of a self-preservation gone wild."[30] In other words, this reading of the project of modernity is the result of a gross *oversimplification*. In this critique, the stance of the calm, collected connoisseur of the force of the better argument is abandoned for the podium of the convinced moralist: "Indeed what is unexplained throughout is their certain lack of concern in dealing with the (to put it in the form of a slogan) achievements of occidental rationalism. *How could these two men of the enlightenment (which they both remain) be so unappreciative of the rational content of cultural modernity, that all they perceive everywhere is a binding of reason and domination, of power and validity?* Have they also let themselves be inspired by Nietzsche in drawing their criteria for cultural criticism from a basic experience of aesthetic modernity that has now been *rendered independent?*"[31] Habermas, of course, answers the question in the affirmative.

Whether or not this argument against the concentration on aesthetic modernity works, and I have reason to suggest later that it does not, this kind of argument reveals much about about the current strategy of Jürgen

---

[30] Ibid., p. 168.
[31] Ibid., p. 182. (Emphasis mine.)

Habermas's thought. What must surely strike one who casually opens *The Philosophical Discourse of Modernity* is the extraordinary pretension of the work, to take on the world as it were. One comes to understand that this is no mock battle; rather, its author is deadly serious. This relatively brief look at the work (I will leave the most controversial parts on Heidegger, Derrida and Foucault until later) suggests a certain strategy for what I have characterized as an attempt to retrieve the project of modernity.

In *The Philosophical Discourse of Modernity* Habermas has developed essentially two arguments against those who, like himself, either attempt to retrieve the project of modernity or, unlike himself, attempt to abandon it. The first argument, which we shall call the reduction to the philosophy of the subject argument, attempts to interpret all forms of rationality as expressions of the dilemmas of self-consciousness which can be resolved by self-consciousness. As we saw in the case of Hegel, such an argument fails because it reduces a plurality of interests to the monadological interests of an absolute self-consciousness. We saw the argument presented in its minimalist form. As we shall come to see, the argument is much more complex and has a more universal application. The second argument, which I call the oversimplification argument, presumes that certain philosophical orientations, particularly those of the counter-enlightenment, claim one sphere of the "differentiated" experience of modernity as representative of a certain form of rationality at the expense of the others. Again, we have seen this argument only in its minimalist form. It will take on much larger proportions as we go on.

One thing is obvious. This form of argumentation bears the trace of a certain strategy. The strategy can be fairly easily linked with nineteenth-century German thought, where at least certain thinkers found it necessary to summarize the tradition in order to go beyond it, through a kind of "immanent critique."[32] This strategy works to the extent that the arguments developed for its purposes are sound. Certainly, the strategy places a large share of the burden, not on those critiqued, but on the claim that the arguments proposed are valid. In other words, this strategy draws attention to itself, having made the rather outrageous claim that all the other marchers in the grand parade of philosophical reason are out of step.

This discussion began with the suggestion that there was a certain

---

[32] I want to be extremely cautious here. It would be unfair to put Habermas in the so-called *Meisterdenker* tradition. But it seems important to point out that the claims of this "systematic" position are not modest. Habermas, over the years, has been careful to limit the claims of his position. For a look at one of the more recent statements summarizing his view of what philosophy should be and do it would be advisable to look at the essay, "Philosophy as Stand-in and Interpreter," in *After Philosophy*, eds Baynes, K., Bohman, J., and McCarthy, T. (Cambridge, MA, The MIT Press, 1987), pp. 296–318.

tension between the project of modernity and the philosophy of language. As one could have anticipated, the overall strategy adopted by Habermas is to retrieve the project of modernity through a highly specialized form of the philosophy of language, a form which presumably will do precisely what could not be done in the older context of the philosophy of consciousness. However, and this is the question, can the philosophy of language be tailored to the project of modernity, without resorting to the old dilemmas of the philosophy of consciousness?

2
The Strategy of the Theory of Communicative Action

The rather startling premise for the project of the theory of communicative action and for the book bearing that title is not only that language as communicative discourse is *emancipatory*,[1] but also that communicative forms of discourse have a certain priority over other forms of linguistic usage. With this thesis Habermas will claim not only to lead us out of the desert of the philosophy of consciousness to the more fruitful realm of the philosophy of language, but also, to outwit the dialectic of enlightenment to which prior theory has, as we have seen, in one way or another succumbed. In so doing, Habermas will have us entertain a thesis as old as enlightenment thought itself, namely, that Western rationality is emancipatory. But he will have us re-read that thesis as one freed from the strictures of the philosophy of the subject fundamental to the philosophy of consciousness. In other words, his reading of the twentieth-century transition to the philosophy of language suggests that instead of philosophy of language doing things differently, it does things better.[2]

This is a highly controversial claim which both follower and critic will want to put to the test.[3] One could construct alternative scenarios regarding the uses and abuses of the contemporary transition to the philosophy of language. One scenario might argue from the developments in linguistics as paradigmatic for the philosophy of language. Using Ferdinand de

---

[1] In principle, Habermas attempts to read his emancipation thesis out of a claim about the nature of discourse rather than out of political theory. The emancipation thesis will then rest upon a scientific assertion about the nature of language. This, as we shall see, enables him to sustain the emancipatory thesis free from a claim based on epistemology.

[2] The issue here is one of defining the prerogatives of the philosophy of language. The terms "different" and "better" in this sentence suggest the particular path to be followed by the philosophy of language. Philosophy of language is not interpreted here necessarily as a different way of doing philosophy. Consequently, it has roughly the same subject matter as the old philosophy of consciousness which preceded it. Hence, the philosophy of language is perceived in the mold of the philosophy of consciousness. Philosophy of language does not have a different subject matter, rather it has a better method of resolving traditional philosophical problems. As we will see immediately, this way of approaching the philosophy of language is not without problems.

[3] This is controversial because the philosophy of language seems to be designed for the same program that was heretofore reserved for the philosophy of consciousness.

Saussure's[4] distinction between diachronic and synchronic as fundamental, diachronic historical-evolutionary schemes for understanding language follow the model of the enlightenment, while synchronic a-historical systems isolate language from time, seeing it as a structure of internal relations. The discovery of synchronicity of language led to the undermining of the older historical-evolutionary view. The resulting view would be that the project of modernity and a philosophy based on language would not be correlative inasmuch as the emancipatory principle could not be associated with a specific temporally discernable form of linguistic apprehension. Language could be said to be emancipatory, but emancipation need not be associated with modernity. From this point of view an attempt to link the project of modernity with the philosophy of language could be said to be anachronistic. Certainly, pre-twentieth-century linguistics could quite easily be correlated with the project of modernity because it conceived of itself diachronically. Hence, the historical study of language was associated with an evolutionary model which assumed language to evolve both in character and complexity. However, once it was discovered that language is universally complex regardless of occasion, i.e., an archaic language can be as complex as a modern one, and further, once it was discovered that getting behind language to a pre-linguistic level was pure conjecture, the evolutionary model for understanding language had to be abandoned on scientific grounds. This did not mean that language could not be studied diachronically, but it did mean that most of the value assumptions associated with diachronicity had to be given up. From this perspective, Habermas's attempt to retrieve the project of modernity through language would be much closer to the older diachronic model for the understanding of language. In principle, there is nothing wrong with that attempt except that it seems at the outset difficult to validate such an understanding of language. According to the problematic of modernity, as deciphered by Habermas, such a claim must be presented with a certain validity in order to avoid the potential error of basing arguments on pre-modern theoretical construction, i.e. to have failed to develop the structure of normativity out of itself, and to fall back upon a false utopia. No doubt, this undertaking depends upon a certain conception of what philosophy can and cannot do.

I   The Role of Reconstructive Science

In theory construction, Habermas is either at his eclectic best or his systematic worst, depending on where in the spectrum of modern or

---

[4] Ferdinand de Saussure, *Course in General Linguistics* (NewYork, McGraw-Hill 1959). From the 1906–11 lectures in Geneva.

postmodern philosophy one stands. After all, the theory of communicative action is just that, a theory, which attempts to tailor a very specific kind of philosophy of language to the project of modernity. Of course, the very suggestion that philosophy involve itself in theory construction is controversial. There are those who would prefer to leave the construction of theory to the sciences, while seeing philosophy involved in tasks of either therapy or edification.[5] Modernity presented philosophy with its two most difficult problems, both of which have been rejected by postmodern philosophy, namely, the attempt to provide foundations for knowledge and the attempt to determine and limit the diverse areas of inquiry. Richard Rorty's critique of Habermas is rather suggestive in this regard inasmuch as he pointed out some time ago that the so-called "Kantian grid" shines through in his philosophy. He meant, of course, that there was a certain nostalgia for foundationalism, the obsession of the *Meisterdenker*, present in Habermas's quest to establish clear and certain domains for philosophical investigation.[6] Rorty had the appendix to *Knowledge and Human Interests*[7] in mind, where the domains of the various sciences were established.

Although Habermas has not recanted his position in response to this critique, he has augmented it by claiming a place for science as reconstructive science.[8] For Habermas the problem begins with Kant. "In championing the idea of a cognition before cognition, Kantian philosophy sets up a domain between itself and the sciences, arrogating authority to itself. It wants to clarify the foundations of the sciences once and for all, defining the limits of what can and cannot be experienced. This is tantamount to an act of ushering the sciences to their proper place."[9] In this view, the term "usher" refers to the "foundationalism of epistemology" which Kantian philosophy claims to establish. This is the first flaw. The second is equally problematic:

---

[5] Here I have in mind developments in modern philosophy from the later Wittgenstein to Gadamer and Rorty, which would conceive of the claims of the philosophy of language in non-systematic terms.

[6] Richard Rorty, *Philosophy and the Mirror of Nature* (Princeton, NJ, Princeton University Press, 1979) pp. 379–85.

[7] Jürgen Habermas, *Knowledge and Human Interests* (Boston, Beacon Press, 1971), pp. 301–17.

[8] Jürgen Habermas, "Philosophy as Stand-in and Interpreter," in *After Philosophy*, eds. Baynes, Bohman and McCarthy (Cambridge, The MIT Press, 1987), pp. 296–318. From "Philosophie als Platzhalter und Interpret" in *Moralbewusstsein und kommunikatives Handeln* (Frankfurt am Main, Suhrkamp, 1983). This is the point where Habermas attempts to answer Rorty's rather astute criticism regarding his (Habermas's) reliance on and use of a Kantian epistemological foundation.

[9] Ibid., p. 297.

Kant replaces the substantive concept of reason, found in traditional metaphysics, with a concept of reason, the moments of which have undergone differentiation to the point where their unity is merely formal. He sets up practical reason, judgment, and theoretical cognition in isolation from each other, giving each a foundation unto itself, with the result that philosophy is cast in the role of the highest arbiter for all matters, including culture as a whole. Kantian philosophy differentiates what Weber was to call the "value spheres of culture" (science and technology, law and morality, art and art criticism), while at the same time legitimating them within their respective limits. Thus Kant's philosophy poses as the highest court of appeal vis-à-vis the sciences and culture as a whole.[10]

Here, it is said, philosophy assumes the role of judge. Both Rorty and Habermas agree that the role of usher and judge are "too much" for philosophy to assume. In the process of giving up these roles, Rorty argues that philosophy ought also to give up being the "guardian of rationality." Habermas disagrees.[11] The task becomes one of carving out a more modest role[12] for philosophy while sustaining some of its original claims. In the place of usher, the epistemological role, Habermas conceives of the role of stand-in (*Platzhalter*). Here, Habermas slightly redefines the classical-modern relationship of philosophy and science. Instead of assuming with Kant, as he did earlier in *Knowledge and Human Interests*, that philosophy relates to science as its foundational critic, here he conceives of the philosopher as the surrogate for the reconstructive scientist.[13] "Whose seat would philosophy be keeping, what would it be standing in for?" Habermas asks. And the answer: "Empirical theories with strong universalistic claims."[14] In the place of judge, Habermas submits the role of interpreter. Here, the argument is that philosophy doesn't have to differentiate and appropriately limit the various spheres of modern life, differentiation is rather to be a modern "given." "The sons and daughters of modernity have progressively learned to differentiate their cultural tradition in terms of

[10] Ibid., pp. 297–8.

[11] At this point the differences between Rorty and Habermas, i.e. the differences between a philosophy which has edification as its aim and one which has more systematic pretensions, begin to emerge.

[12] A more modest role than Habermas had heretofore conceived.

[13] Reconstructive science is to be distinguished from ordinary science by its peculiar combination of empirical scientific understanding with philosophic generalization or universalization. The works of Freud or Piaget provide examples. "Starting primarily from the intuitive knowledge of competent subjects — competent in terms of judgment, action, and language — and secondarily from systematic knowledge handed down by culture, the reconstructive sciences explain the presumably universal bases of rational experience and judgment, as well as of action and linguistic communication." Ibid., p. 310.

[14] Ibid.

these three aspects of rationality such that they deal with issues of truth, justice and taste discretely, never simultaneously."[15] With this kind of sophisticated differentiation, the spheres of cultural modernity have become ever more distinct, ever more autonomous. While giving up claims of totality, philosophy can act as a mediator, adjudicating between the competitive interests of the various spheres, searching for the "lost unity of reason" which today's "expert cultures" have lost.

Reaching understanding in the lifeworld requires a cultural tradition that ranges across the whole spectrum, not just the fruits of science and technology. As far as philosophy is concerned, it might do well to refurbish its link with the totality by taking on the role of interpreter on behalf of the lifeworld. It might then be able to help set in motion the interplay between the cognitive-instrumental, moral-practical, and aesthetic-expressive dimensions that has come to a standstill today, like a tangled mobile.[16]

As we witness the ensuing drama, we will want to see to what extent the emancipatory potential of reason can be discovered within language and redeemed as a claim resting on the insights of reconstructive science. The tension between the philosophy of language and the project of modernity manifests itself here. On the one hand, it is necessary to construct a theory of language that is scientific, in the sense of reconstructive science; on the other hand it is essential that such theory be correlative with the project of modernity as Habermas has defined it. In order to fulfill the latter condition it will be necessary to construct a theory of language which is essentially diachronic in character. But the diachronic perspective on language may prove to be an unscientific and highly prejudiced way of looking at it. If overcoming the diachronic view leads to a new scientific paradigm with consequences for understanding language, the argument for the retention of the older, diachronic paradigm as scientific may appear spurious. The theory of communicative action, as a consequence, represents a kind of struggle, namely, to render scientific that very theory which could be conceived quite differently in the course of historical development.

Habermas assumes that there is a kind of scientific reconstruction to be teased out of speech-act theory which can retrieve the emancipatory poten-

[15] Ibid., p. 312. This reflects the return of Habermas's earlier preoccupation with the tripartite division of knowledge under a different form. Significantly, at this point the divisions of knowledge can be attributed to common sense under the inspiration of Weber's concept of spheres of value rather than to epistemological grounding as in the case of *Knowledge and Human Interests*. No doubt this transformation reflects a rather convenient turn of events given the current difficulties attributed to epistemological grounding.

[16] Ibid., p. 313. The image is a fascinating one. We shall have occasion to refer to it again later. Significantly, the image is not a logical but an aesthetic one.

tials of reason while avoiding the difficulties to which theory had been subject in the past. Here, of course, philosophy claims to be the stand-in for science. Whether or not one can claim that the result is an empirical theory "with strong universalistic claims" remains to be seen. In any case, that is precisely what the theory of communicative action attempts to become, namely, a quasi-scientific theory and not a venture in foundationalist epistemology.

II Toward a Theory of Communicative Action

(a) Critical Perspectives

In the book, *The Theory of Communicative Action*, Habermas's venture in reconstructive science follows two procedures, the historical critique of theory and the subsequent reconstruction of that theory. The ostensible subject of the book's inquiry is Max Weber's sociological theory of rationalization seen through the paradigm of the philosophy of consciousness.[17] Inasmuch as Weber influenced the best of modern Western Marxist social theory, this dialogue becomes a kind of fascinating adventure as we witness the greats of the socio-philosophical tradition fall one by one, clustered at his feet. This reading of Weber's view of the history of rationalization plays on his well-known attempt to interpret the history of the West as a kind of drama in which a certain form of rationality and rational action triumph, while negatively it extends from the judgment that this form of rationality results in a certain impoverishment of the human species.

According to Weber, the institutional bearer of this form of rationality was capitalism, and the specific form of rationalization was purposive rational action. Habermas claims that the best of theoretical Marxism from Lukács through Adorno and Horkheimer took its point of departure from Weber's theory of rationalization. Lukács's reconstruction of Marx, based on his attempt to extend the notion of commodity fetishism to the concept of reification of the thought processes of bourgeois society, depends, in this view, on the Weberian insight that the dominant form of rationality to

[17] The basic assumption at this point is that the sociological and the philosophical projects can be brought together in such a manner that social theory according to Weber and company can be integrated with a philosophical theory conceived as a theory of rationality. The claim that Weber's analysis is flawed by being beholden to the rubrics and categories of the philosophy of consciousness follows from this wager. This entire strategy represents a decision made in the seventies to bring together the sociological or social-theoretical and the philosophical projects which have constituted the two poles of Habermas's work. For an excellent analysis of the work of Jürgen Habermas which concentrates on the integration of the two fields of activity, see: Helga Gripp, *Jürgen Habermas*, (Paderborn, Schoningh, 1984), pp. 72–106.

emerge in capitalist society was purposive rational action, a form of rational action which resulted in the loss of meaning and freedom. According to Lukács this process was associated with subjective reason to which he juxtaposed objective reason as a positive alternative. In this view, Lukács's reconstruction of Marx resulted in a step back to objective idealism; to its theory of history and totality. Taking the process a step further, Horkheimer, with the benefit of Lukács's reconstruction of Weber's theory, was able to rename purposive rational action as "instrumental rationality."

Adorno and Horkheimer tried to generalize their understanding to account for all civilizational processes, but they were more skeptical about returning to absolute idealism. What Lukács tried to do through Hegel's logic, they tried to do empirically. They did not try to read a form of thought out of the commodity as Lukács did; instead they found their type of reification in the form of the existence of the species, a discovery which led to the extraordinary role that nature − instincts, repression, ego-identity, and so on − would play in their theories. In this reading, the peculiarity of the theory is said to be that the critique of reason leads to the use of *mimesis* in which the cipher is said to be the disclosure of truth. Hence, the irony: they must deal with the great tradition in philosophy and yet within that tradition objective reason discloses itself as ideology. The conclusion of the argument is that they are condemned to go back and forth forever between subjective and objective reason.[18]

For the sake of analysis, this entire reading of Weber can be reduced to a simple "if−then" proposition: if Weber can be shown to be wrong, then the best of post-Marx Marxian social theory is also wrong. The entire weight of the proposition is based on the "if" clause. If Weber is wrong? Weber's analysis can be catagorized rather neatly. After all, the iron cage analogy originated from his pen. Western rationality reduced to its instrumental core has no further prospects for regenerating itself. Weber's dire reading of the Western rationalization process is based on an understanding of reason and rationalization in relationship to secularization. As secularization processes develop, they eat away at the core of regenerative reason leading to the ultimate reduction, *Zweckrationalität*.

Significantly, and this is Habermas's claim, the assumption stated above regarding the rationalization process is shown to be false not simply because of a faulty hermeneutic with regard to the history of Western rationalization processes, but because of the dilemma in the very understanding of the function of rationalization itself, namely, the conceptualization of reason in terms of subject−object relations. The problem is not merely a hermeneutic

---

[18] See Jürgen Habermas, *The Theory of Communicative Action*, vol. 1, tr. Thomas McCarthy (Boston, Beacon Press, 1984), pp. 339−402.

one, rather it is logical.[19] It may be interesting, but it is not necessary to argue with Weber's historical analysis. Weber and those who read social theory through instrumental categories are said to be part of a larger problem. Hence, one can say that Weber is wrong regarding his interpretation of the history of Western rationalization processes because he conceived of things instrumentally. But, as one comes to discover, that is not really the issue. The proposition can be stated differently. *Weber conceived of things instrumentally because he conceived of them in terms of subject—object relations.* Hence, the real issue regarding the interpretation of Weber and company is the second assumption, namely, that to *conceive of things in terms of subject—object relations amounts to conceiving them in terms of instrumental reason.*[20]

The second assumption results in the claim that the dilemmas of instrumental reason cannot be effectively conceived and resolved within the context of a philosophy of consciousness, or, to put it more simply, all subject—object formulations are instrumental. This leads to the very interesting proposition that a critique of instrumental reason developed within the confines of a philosophy of consciousness will be unable to free itself from the very instrumentalism implicit in the subject—object formulation. If that is the case, critical theory formulated under the problematic of the philosophy of consciousness is dead. But that is the case if and only if all philosophy of consciousness formulations are destined to be thought of instrumentally. Ultimately, this is the assumption of the theory of communicative action. From the point of view of the rationality problematic, this amounts to claiming that reason, when generating its own structures for action and contemplation, is limited by instrumentality. This formulation entered into modern philosophy of consciousness with Hobbes. Endeavors were made to overcome it, but they are to be classified under the category of the "metaphysics of reconciliation."[21] All attempts at reformulating the original materialist problematic as it was established by Hobbes, with reason under the banner of self-interest, all endeavors to set up a theory of intersubjectivity as established by Hegel's concept of recognition, as well as Marx's concept of labor, are more or less doomed to failure. The real enemy in the theory of communicative action is not Weber, Lukács,

---

[19] The general assumption is that a sociological program can be subject to a philosophical critique according to a specific theory of rationality.

[20] Here, it would follow, lies the hidden, unexamined assumption of earlier critical theory, namely, that the very use of instrumental reason presupposes a subject—object formulation.

[21] The most interesting attempts to move beyond instrumental formulation were undertaken by Hegel, with whom one may associate the idea of a "metaphysics of reconciliation." Unfortunately, according to this analysis, that attempt also failed because it too was limited to a subject—object formulation.

Horkheimer or Adorno *per se*, but post-Cartesian philosophy of consciousness in general which was left with the concept of a completely isolated
subject whose relationship to the world can be only instrumentally conceived
and not intersubjectively established. To follow the argument: one can only
get to that which the philosophy of consciousness wanted if one turns in a
semantic direction. "One only gets hold of that relation-to-self that has
traditionally been thematized and distorted — as self-consciousness if one
extends the line of inquiry in a pragmatic direction. There it is the analysis
of the meaning of the performative — and not the referential — use of the
expression 'I' within the system of personal pronouns that offers a pro-
mising approach to the problematic of self-consciousness."[22]

(b) Toward a Constructive View

If the theory of communicative action is to succeed as a theory it must be
able to resolve the dilemmas of the philosophy of consciousness. The
question for the interpreter is: can Habermas's version of the philosophy of
language do this? In order to resolve the dilemma of instrumental reason an
entire philosophy of language is put forth, the elements of which are an
account of the origins of language, an elaboration of speech-act theory, a
theory of the three-fold structure of discourse, and a concept of the
relationship between language and the lifeworld.

The claim that communicative forms are primary is the principal claim
upon which the theory of language rests.[23] There are two fundamental
reasons for stating this: first, the entire analysis of Weber, Lukács, and
critical theory presumed and indeed attempted to show that the reading of
the history of rationalization in the West was false because it failed to
construct any real alternatives to *Zweckrationalität*. Secondly, as I have
shown, this assumption is derived from the more general one that all
versions of the philosophy of consciousness were subject to the same
"instrumental" reduction. If the case can be made for the primacy of
communicative forms of action, it will be possible to overcome not only
Weber, Lukács and critical theory, but, and perhaps this is more important,
the dilemmas of the philosophy of consciousness as well.

Strategically, the argument for the paradigm shift to the philosophy of
language is a very specific one. It is worth noting that the philosophy of
language in other and earlier Anglo-American formulations was not given
the distinctive task of uniting the project of modernity with the philosophy

---

[22] Ibid., p. 397.
[23] This is certainly the most fundamental claim of the entire corpus that constitutes the
work of the later Habermas. The assumption behind it is that communicative claims are
somehow emancipatory.

of language. Indeed, the issue of instrumental vs non-instrumental linguistic usage among ordinary language philosophers in general and speech-act theorists in particular is not a burning one.[24] The originators of speech-act theory had no such distinction in mind upon the construction of their version of the philosophy of language. I point this out to make it clear that appeal to the philosophy of language *per se* does not suffice to resolve the rationality problematic which arises out of the philosophy of consciousness. Actually, one might assume that the philosophy of language is as riddled with instrumental usage as the previous paradigm. This takes nothing away from Habermas's argument. However, it does make it clear that it is only by the force of a distinctive argument regarding the philosophy of language that the dilemma of instrumental reason can be resolved. Appeal to the philosophy of language as such makes little difference regarding the instrumentality of subject–object usage because there is no automatic relationship between language and emancipation. Hence, the entire weight of the argument for the paradigm shift from the philosophy of consciousness to the communicative conception of language should be placed directly on the shoulders of its originator.

Let us follow the argument for a moment. The first assumption is that action can take two forms, namely, strategic action and communicative action. The former would include purposive–rational action while action aimed at reaching an understanding would be communicative. Communicative action is non-instrumental in the following sense: "A communicatively achieved agreement has a rational basis; it cannot be imposed by either party, whether instrumentally through intervention in the situation directly or strategically through influencing decisions of opponents."[25] Such an action has implicit within it a validity claim which is in principle criticizable, i.e., the person to whom it is addressed can respond either "yes" or "no" based on reasons. Communicative actions are in this sense foundational, they cannot, it is said, be reducible to teleological actions. If they were, one would be back precisely in the problematic of the philosophy of consciousness.

However, a second question arises: is there a way to show that communicative action cannot be reduced to strategic action? Habermas argues: "This will turn out not to be the case if it can be shown that the use of language with an orientation to reaching an understanding is the *original mode* of language use, upon which indirect understanding, giving something

---

[24] Whether one turns to the later Wittgenstein or Searle, it does not appear that the distinction between instrumental and non-instrumental usage which was essential to interpretations of the school of critical theory both early and late was important as a fundamental category of interpretation.

[25] Ibid., p. 287.

to understand or letting something be understood, and the instrumental use of language in general, are parasitic."[26] In order to make this case, Habermas relies on an interpretation of Austin's distinction between illocutionary and perlocutionary discourse. Illocutionary discourse is said to be communicative while perlocutionary discourse is essentially strategic.

This thesis regarding the primacy of the communicative mode constitutes the major theoretical insight sustaining the entire edifice Habermas has built. In a very specific sense it is intended to provide a solution to the "rationality problematic" spoken of earlier. If one can show that communicative forms are by nature prior to instrumental or strategic forms, then the earlier interpretation of modes of rationality as represented by Weber and others can be dismissed as false. Equally, one can show how this discursive form of rationality came to take the place of earlier, non-discursive, mythic forms of rationality. Further, one can demonstrate the essentially regenerative power of reason without recourse to historical argument. In other words, the thesis regarding the primacy of communicative over strategic forms functions as an hypothesis of reconstructive science. *The argument is not that communicative forms ought to be primary, the argument is that they are primary. Reason does not need to be regenerated, it is by nature regenerative in the sense that reason as communicative reason is embedded in language.*[27]

Certainly, it is striking how effectively this thesis works within the later theoretical development of Habermas's work. If it could be said that every great philosophy is based on a single simple (but not simplistic) idea, this would be it. The theory of modernity, the theory of evolution, the discourse ethics, the theory of the origin and development of language, the concepts of politics and law — all can be systematically derived from this fundamental thesis. However, and this is the difficulty, the thesis regarding the primacy of communication must be demonstrated. One cannot simply appeal to Austin; Austin's theory must be reconstructed to demonstrate the thesis. Neither can one appeal to the later developments of speech-act theory since it is now even less concerned with the communication thesis than it was at the time of the writing of *The Theory of Communicative Action.*[28] Further, as suggested previously, appeal to ordinary language philosophy is even less successful inasmuch as it provides no conclusive evidence regarding the primacy of the communicative over the strategic. Hence, there is no court of appeal to which one can turn which demonstrates

---

[26] Ibid., pp. 288–92. See discussion.

[27] Habermas conceives of the philosophy of language as a theory of rationality. That is why the problematic of rationality and rationalization can be resolved at the level of language.

[28] I refer to Searle's more recent turn toward problems of intentionality in relationship to speech act theory.

unequivocally the thesis regarding the primacy of communication. Hence, we are dealing with an argument. An argument constructed by Habermas, with the help of assumptions developed and shared by Karl-Otto Apel, but just the same an argument which has no universal community of scholars to which it can appeal for its evidential truth.

If the above is the case, the ball is definitely in Habermas's court. The question is, can he knock it out with sufficient force to impress his interpreters? There is a sense in which the appeal to the linguistic paradigm is brought forth shrouded in the magic of scientific discovery; that new bit of information so cruelly withheld from Habermas's predecessors in social theory. However, our skeptic might point out that the attempt to resolve the problems of Continental philosophy with the tools of analytic philosophy has not been an easy one. Indeed, there have been brilliant syntheses. To be sure, there have been genuine attempts to demonstrate common origins.[29] Today, there has been a genuine interpenetration of one by the other. But appeal to the linguistic paradigm in the form of speech-act theory does not directly resolve anything without a serious attempt at reconstruction.[30]

If, in fact, the appeal to the linguistic paradigm is presented for what it is − grounded in a very specialized argument to be taken as reconstructive science − then one is in a position to follow the path of the argument developed in the course of the past several years. Indeed, the arguments based on the thesis supporting the primacy of communicative action emerge before the interpreter like segments of a spreading Chinese fan. There is the argument from the three-fold structure of language which tries, on the basis of the Weberian-Kantian insight regarding differentiation, to conceive the tripartite structure of linguistic usage − scientific, moral, aesthetic − from the perspective of modalities of communication. There is the argument for the formation of the lifeworld as the linguistic and communicative backdrop for the intervention and rationalization of more strategic media. There is the argument for a discourse ethics to be based on the fundamental insights regarding communication *via* justification. Of course, the overall purpose of this venture into a form of the philosophy of language is to legitimate the project of modernity with its basic assumption about the principle of emancipation in forms of linguistic interaction as a scientific claim.

---

[29] I refer to those attempts to interpret Wittgenstein's Continental origins.

[30] The issue mentioned here, namely, the particular reading of Continental philosophy developed by Habermas, is one to which I will return in the final chapter. Habermas wants to resolve a particular problematic with the tools of analytic philosophy, a problematic derived from his particular way of reading modern Continental philosophy.

III Communication as First Philosophy
The Contribution of Karl-Otto Apel

Just how plausible is the thesis that the originary mode of language is communicative? If the thesis is true, given the overall framework of the Habermasian enterprise, the great dilemmas encountered in a comprehensive reflection on the history of theory would be overcome. The communication thesis is not merely the notion of communicative competence as taken from Chomsky. Rather, the claim that the originary mode of language is a communicative, as opposed to a stategic one, presupposes a contrafactual communicative community which is by nature ideally predisposed to refrain from instrumental forms of domination. Hence, the assertion of communicative over strategic forms of discursive interaction presupposes a certain political form of association which is the guarantor of a form of progressive emancipation. If one can claim that the originary mode of discourse is emancipatory, then not only are the dilemmas of instrumental reason overcome but the project of modernity, with its attempt to overcome the dialectic of enlightenment, is secure. It is secure in the sense that the principle of emancipation need not be established as an "ought," as the claim of an ancient eschatological or utopian scheme, but rather rests firmly on the fertile soil of reconstructive science. The claims of the great emancipatory thinkers from Hegel to the present, all of which can be said to have been undermined, can be redeemed and with them the project of modernity. Indeed, one must marvel at this attempt to outwit the dialectic of enlightenment. But is it plausible? Can the philosophy of language be formulated in such a way as to agree with the project of modernity?

One answer might be to read the history of philosophy from the point of view of the communication thesis seeing a coalescence between the development of philosophy and the move toward communication. In an article entitled "The Transcendental Conception of Language-Communication and the Idea of First Philosophy,"[31] Karl-Otto Apel does precisely that. Apel speculates in the following way: "One could — and, as I think, one should — wonder whether in our day philosophy of language has in fact taken over the role of a *First Philosophy* which was ascribed (attributed) to Ontology by Aristotle and later claimed for *Epistemology or Transcendental Philosophy* in the sense of Kant."[32] Although the arguments regarding Aristotle and Kant are interesting, the highlight of the article is the transformation of Wittgenstein's idea of the "language game," the idea which

---

[31] Karl-Otto, Apel "The Transcendental Conception of Language Communication and the Idea of a First Philosophy" in *The History of Linguistic Thought and Contemporary Linguistics*, ed. Herman Parret (Berlin and New York, DeGruyter, 1976), pp. 32–61.

[32] Ibid., p. 32.

destroyed the possibility of there being a private language, into the transcendental conception of language-communication. According to this argument, the condition for the possibility of there being a language game is the presupposition of an ideal language game which in turn would involve the communication community.

It is this ideal language game, not yet realized in the factual language games, that, in my opinion, is presupposed, although counterfactually, as condition for the possibility and validity for *understanding* human forms of life: it is at least implicitly anticipated in all human actions claiming to be meaningful and it is explicitly anticipated in philosophical arguments claiming to be valid. I would like to call this ideal language game which can justify Wittgenstein's thesis of the impossibility of a "private language" the *transcendental language game* which would correspond to the idea of a *communicative competence* of man in the sense of a *universal or transcendental pragmatics of* language-communication.[33]

Hence, a communicative assumption would exist as the condition for the possibility of there being any kind of linguistic expression in the sense of a language game. Apel would then not necessarily show how communicative forms could be established over strategic forms of discourse, but he does show how a theory of communicative action would be the basis for an understanding of the philosophy of language.[34]

Apel's approach is different from Wittgenstein's in the sense that language use refers not simply to language itself but also to the communicative community which decides about language usage. This is, in Apel's words, to postulate the *"indefinite ideal communication community,"* along with the *"transcendental language game,"* a postulation which amounts to using "Wittgenstein against Wittgenstein." Indeed, this use of Wittgenstein against Wittgenstein becomes something like standing Wittgenstein on his feet as Marx claimed to have done to Hegel. Proper linguistic usage is not referable to the internal structure of language *per se*, but to the level of competence achieved by the communication community which can be looked at from the perspective of different stages of development. Hence, the principle of development (evolution) which Wittgenstein thought he had so successfully undermined, rises from the debris of the philosophical past to again determine the direction of philosophy. "Although a philosophically relevant *definition*, in order to be intelligible, must always be connected with a *given use* of words ... it must nevertheless take account of the newest state of human experience and argumentation, thus anticipating

[33] Ibid., p. 57.
[34] Habermas's argument for the originary character of the communicative over the strategic mode may be regarded as a complement to Apel's.

in a given language game the structure of the ideal language game that could be valid for all rational beings."[35] Hence, the celebrated "linguistic turn" anticipated by developments in modern linguistics and actualized in the philosophy of the later Wittgenstein, turns again, to retrace the development of philosophy as an evolutionary principle. The relativism of Wittgenstein's particular way of looking at language under Apel's reinterpretation is replaced by a post-Kantian universalism which can be connected to an evolutionary history of theory.

Apel acknowledges that, although there are real problems with this view, it is possible to conceive a relationship between the internal system of language and the external game of communication. For example, if it were possible to correlate the internal structure of language with the development of communicative competence, then it would also be necessary to mediate between "syntactico-semantical language-systems and semantico-pragmatic language games." Apel acknowledges that it was not always possible to do this. However – and now comes the linchpin of the entire Apelian edifice – scientific evolution may solve the problem: "And the historical progress of communication in the pragmatic dimension may even influence the semantical component of languages notwithstanding its dependence on different system structures."[36] Precisely this prospect most endears itself to Apel. The consequence of this view would be that the structure of the so-called natural languages would not be independent of their pragmatic interpretation. If anything, this proposed mediation owes itself to the development of science. Indeed, if in archaic culture the system of language could be juxtaposed to the so-called form of life, this may no longer be the case, precisely because of the development of science and technology. "The variety of language-games as parts of forms of life has not disappeared; it has been superformed or played over, so to speak, by the language game of science and technology which, in spite of its own complexity, has brought about something like the unity of a form of life."[37] Hence, if this is the case, the unity between the semantic and the pragmatic can be postulated. Also, inasmuch as forms of life are correlative with semantic structures, one could reconstruct their evolution as the condition for the possibility of analyzing the potential claims of language. Although Apel doesn't follow this option, Habermas does.[38]

If one applies this conception of the unity between the semantic and the

[35] Ibid., p. 58.
[36] Ibid., p. 60.
[37] Ibid., p. 59.
[38] Habermas's attempt to develop both an ontogenetic and a philogenetic theory of evolution, particularly in the second volume of *The Theory of Communicative Action*, indicates his commitment to this option.

pragmatic to the problem of first philosophy, the history of philosophy can be reinterpreted from the point of view of language communication, not by envisioning an end of philosophy as Wittgenstein does, but rather as a redemption of the initial claims of philosophy. The Greeks, having failed to understand that the concepts are derived from the use of words, reduced the question of meaning to "extra linguistic entities." "First philosophy thus far seemed only to be a matter of the 'Logos' and its onto-logical relations to the 'essence' of things."[39] With the change in direction inaugurated by Cartesian philosophy, first philosophy focused on con-sciousness as the extra-linguistic entity to which all meaning could be reduced. According to Apel, it is not that we should give up on the age-old problems of "essence" and "meaning," rather the transition to the *a priori* of language communication will shed a new light on them. Indeed, this last major transition in the history of philosophy holds the prospect for the retrieval of the age-old dilemmas of Western thought.

Apel concludes: "The *transcendental* conception of language-communi-cation on the level of pragmatics or hermeneutics may show that, notwith-standing the indispensable mediation of meanings – and hence of all personal intentions – by the use of language, the ancient postulate of intersubjectively valid concepts of the essence of things may be fulfilled in the long run by the process of communication in the indefinite communi-cation-community of rational beings, which was intended and also brought along in all civilized language-communities by the invention of discussion by concepts."[40]

Although Apel and Habermas would disagree on both questions of ultimate justification[41] and the the use of the term transcendental to describe the universal conditions presupposed in language communication, Apel provides a larger framework within which Habermas's view can be located. It is as if Habermas has tailored Apel's general approach to the philosophy of language to meet his more specific requirements. Although Apel's approach does not directly account for the priority of communicative modes over strategic modes of discourse, it does show how the communi-cation thesis could become the dominant mode for the interpretation of major problems in the history of philosophy. First of all, Apel provides a reading of the philosophy of language which, esoteric though it may be, attempts to show how the dilemmas of mainstream philosophy, which has in prior epochs operated outside the realm of language, may be redeemed

---

[39] Ibid., p. 61.
[40] Ibid.
[41] I refer to the debate between Habermas and Apel over the "*Begründungsproblem*" and the possibility of a "*Letztbegründung*" as supported by Apel. See W. Kuhlman, ed. *Moralität und Sittlichkeit* (Frankfurt am Main, Suhrkamp, 1986), p. 10.

in general through a theory of language communication. Second, Apel shows how forms of life which were external to linguistic systems can affect the internal structure of language.

Habermas, with regard to the first achievement, applies Apel's insight to a specific dilemma within philosophy, namely, the project of modernity. For him, the language-communication framework becomes a way of retrieving the project of modernity. Habermas uses the second insight to build the ontogenetic and philogenetic aspects of a theory of evolution based on linguistic communication; a theory which will extend the project of modernity. This latter attempt rounds out the theory of communicative action, expanding the thesis about communication by grounding it in a theory of evolution on the one hand and a critical theory on the other. This may be taken as an exercise in reconstructive science to be understood as a replacement for both Lukács and the Frankfurt school's accounting for processes of reification without capitulating either to Hegelian metaphysics or to instrumental rationality. If successful, it could be labelled a critical science without utopia.

IV Toward the Construction of a Social Theory

Reflections on Mead and Durkheim provide a kind of theoretical bridge to a fully developed theory of communicative action. While Mead is important because of his theory of symbolically mediated interaction, Durkheim is significant because of his analysis of the sacred and the process of secularization of religious norms. From Habermas's point of view, while the former provides further insights for the development of a theory of communicative action, the latter lays a foundation for understanding norm-regulated behavior. One moves procedurally from gesture to symbol to rule to norm. The well-known social psychology of George Herbert Mead postulated interaction based on intersubjective relations. Mead's theory of social consciousness can be, in Habermas's view, nicely integrated with Wittgenstein's theory of rule, showing aspects of communicative competence on the one hand and the social origins of normative behavior on the other. Durkheim's theory of the origins of the sacred in collective consciousness can provide the missing evolutionary link for a theory of norm-regulated behavior. Put simply, Mead's theory of the social constitution of the self and Durkheim's theory of the evolutionary transformation of "rite" from the sacred to the secular go together to provide a kind of double-edged theory of communicative behavior, evolutionary and procedural.

In Habermas's view, the context for this process of the evolutionary development of society, culture and personality is the lifeworld, what Apel would call the form of life correlative with the internal system of language. The lifeworld forms the linguistic context or background for the processes of communication. Through the progressive rationalization of the lifeworld, social change is said to occur. Normal processes of rationalization within the lifeworld are said to occur through communicative action while abnormal processes of change occur through strategic action. Extending Weber's theory of rationalization, one can claim that in the long run, in the course of social development, society can be said to have grown along lines of progressive differentiation and rationalization. This means that as the social system becomes ever more differentiated the lifeworld becomes ever more rationalized. With this goes the controversial claim that social system and lifeworld become ever more differentiated one from another. But as they do each new system development is said to add further life possibilities. The non-realization of these possibilities leads to a counter-emancipation thesis: the taking over of communicative imperatives by strategic imperatives, i.e., the colonization of the lifeworld.

V Conclusion

The point where the project of modernity and the philosophy of language come together in Habermas's work is in the claim that in principle, discourse in its originary form, is emancipatory. To substantiate this controversial claim, Habermas has attempted to retrieve a diachronic reading of language elaborated by the claims of reconstructive science. He has been able to use Apel's reconstruction of the philosophy of language along the lines of first philosophy in two ways: by attempting to retrieve the emancipatory potentials of modernity through following the path from epistemology to language in terms of Apel's rather esoteric reading of the philosophy of language, and by correlating the external structure of the lifeworld with the internal structure of language. The question is, is it plausible?

Early on I argued that there was a certain uneasy tension between the project of modernity and the philosophy of language. The idea of reconstructive science provides the potential for the resolution of this tension between the two seemingly different programs, one being based on the enlightenment principle of emancipation and the other being based on the post-enlightenment discoveries in linguistics and philosophy which defy evolutionary assumptions. The question is: how scientific is the claim that the originary form of discourse is communicative?[42] Further, how scientific is the claim implicit in the scheme shared by Apel and Habermas that as society develops communicative factors play an ever more predominant role to the extent that they affect the internal structure of language itself? Of course, if the apex of linguistic development is the originary communicative mode, i.e., communicative triumphing over strategic imperatives, then it would be possible to construct a philosophy of language which illuminates this thesis and a theory of society which develops the conditions for the emerging communicative thesis.

This is in principle the summation of the Habermasian program. But is this science or is it politics? In the previous chapter we have already seen the Habermasian predilection for the Hegelian political solution to the dilemmas of modernity. Of course, politics, particularly in its modern post-French revolution form, bears the trace of utopia, the secular remnant of the underlying Augustinian eschatological vision of ultimate freedom. In other words, politics lacks justification. To assert a mere political predilection for emancipation would be to fall into the very dilemma that affected those smitten by the dialectic of the enlightenment. So conceived, a giant step forward would be taken if one could effectively and once and for all rest the principle of emancipation on the firm foundation of science, "empirical theories with strong universalistic claims." From this point the questions emerge. Can it be done? Need it be done? Should it be done? Our indefatigable skeptic will want to know about the conditions for its possibility.

---

[42] To anticipate an argument to be taken up in the next chapter, the legitimacy of the derivation of the communication thesis from the nature of language will be questioned. As I will show, there is nothing wrong with the claim that a communicative form of discourse is to be desired; but can that claim be derived from the nature of language? If not, the claims regarding the primacy of the communicative can only be made out of the very contextualism that Habermas criticizes.

3

Problems in The Theory of Communicative Action

If one were to conceive of a situation in which the entire Habermasian edifice constructed in recent years were to be confronted with a single question, none would be more important than the question which addresses the attempt to assert the priority of communicative over other forms of action. Does the communicative thesis hold? Habermas has wanted to show that there is a certain reading of the philosophy of language which will unleash the emancipatory potentials of reason present in discursive acts which are oriented toward reaching an understanding. He has wanted to go a step further by arguing that the communicative orientation is part and parcel of the very nature of language itself, which, when properly investigated, yields the evident priority of communicative over strategic forms of action. He has wanted to claim that the peculiar predilection for the communicative over the strategic is not grounded in a personal preference, in a belief that that is the way things "ought" to be. Rather, he has wanted to ground the communicative thesis in a scientific statement about the nature of discursive interaction.

The reasons are obvious. If he were to base his argument for the primacy of communicative forms of action on personal preference, he would succumb to the same contextualist temptation to which others have succumbed. He too would have dipped from the well of pre-enlightenment tradition. At the same time the position would have a certain arbitrariness, to be potentially tainted with the charge of relativism. Equally, unless discursive action can be seen as communicative in an originary sense, the cynicism which led Weber and company to assert the priority of *Zwechrationalität* as the emerging form of rationality in the modern world could not be reversed. Indeed, as Habermas well knows, there are always utopian sectarians in the modern world whose hopeful visions are shared by members but whose proscriptions are seldom taken seriously by the world at large. It is important that the primacy of communicative forms of discursive interaction be sustained on something more than the moral vision of one meager modern philosopher standing alone in a world which wants to give the hand to instrumentality. Indeed, if the only weapon available is the "force of the better argument" one might hope that it is "better" precisely because it is grounded on something more than hope. Indeed, in this view philosophy must serve as stand-in for science.

I   Critiques of the Communicative Thesis

There are two kinds of criticism of this basic claim that communicative acts are primary. One questions the foundations claimed for the position in speech-act theory, while the other questions the "scientific" status of the claim. Both criticisms are founded in a certain reading of the philosophy of language.

(a)   Communicative vs Strategic Action

With regard to the former point, Jonathan Culler[1] has made a somewhat telling criticism. "Clearly," he writes, "the distinction between communicative action and strategic action is crucial to a pragmatics which would ground the normative force of discourse."[2] Although this issue goes beyond our immediate concern, it is worth pointing out that the designation of communicative action as primary will not only enable Habermas to overcome the weaknesses of those he has criticized, but also to locate further arguments for normativity and validity in the primacy of the communicative form. In other words, the primacy of communicative action will provide the foundation for an ethics grounded in the nature of discourse.[3] As we have seen then, Habermas will need, for a number of reasons including the one just cited, to give to communicative action an "originary" priority. Hence, as we have seen, Habermas will want to grant to communicative action the "originary mode" of linguistic usage from which the strategic use of language is "parasitic."

As Culler suggests, this formulation is not particularly easy to conceptualize. Given the primacy of coming to an understanding in certain instances, one would have to come to an understanding of things before they could act upon the world. Of course, Habermas's primary effort is directed

---

[1] Culler reflects Derrida's critique of speech-act theory. I am not particularly interested in Derrida's claim that there is a certain "latent metaphysics" in speech-act theory. Neither the truth or falsity of that claim, nor the postmodernist assumptions associated with it, are at issue here. Rather, I am interested in the validity of Habermas's claim that within discourse strategic and communicative claims can be dissociated from one another.

[2] Jonathan Culler, "Communicative Competence and Normative Force," *New German Critique*, 35, (Spring/Summer, 1985), p. 135.

[3] The link between the theory of communicative action and the theory of modernity is found in Habermas's assumption that as one can develop a normative reading of modernity, so it is also possible to develop a normative theory of language and discourse. One of the consequences of this association is that a discourse ethics lies hidden within the theory of communicative action as a latent possibility.

toward using Austin's distinction between the perlocutionary and the illocutionary to ground the primacy of the communicative over the strategic.
In Culler's words, "this proves to be an unconvincing move, with little
bearing on the point at issue, which fails in numerous ways: first because
the distinction between the illocutionary and the perlocutionary is not a
distinction between communicative and strategic actions."[4]

Habermas, of course, grounds the communicative in the illocutionary.
Culler's criticism is apt: "Many illocutionary acts seem primarily designed
to produce certain effects rather than to bring about understanding: think
for example, of commanding someone to get out, warning them to look out,
or calling them out, not to mention pronouncing them man and wife or
appointing them to a committee."[5] The point is quite simple: if the perlocutionary has a status equal to the illocutionary, one cannot be derived
from the other.

Actually, according to Austin's usage, many illocutionary acts produce
effects rather than develop understanding. Hence, Culler's rather devastating conclusion: "Since the distinction between illocutionary and perlocutionary acts is not a distinction between communicative and strategic
action, even if one could show the dependency of the perlocutionary on the
illocutionary, it would not advance Habermas's argument."[6]

Habermas might respond that although he uses Austin's argument he
transforms it for his own purposes. Hence, such argument would be
classified as essentially a reconstructive effort regardless of Austin's intentions. However, even then the case would be insufficient because in
order to clearly separate the illocutionary from the perlocutionary one must
demonstrate that they would always be so interpreted *unambiguously*. One
could perhaps do that by anchoring the distinction between the illocutionary
and the perlocutionary in either an intentionalist semantics or a phenomenological notion of intentionality.[7] Habermas, however, is rightfully
wary of such an attempt, considering it a return to epistemological orientations which characterized the philosophy of consciousness.

Culler's second point follows from his first. He writes: "Since it is
difficult to show dependency, Habermas claims that understanding utterances is prior to and independent of understanding purposive activity."[8]
This point refers to Habermas's claim that it is possible to "clarify the

---

[4] Ibid., p. 136.

[5] Ibid.

[6] Ibid.

[7] But that course has already been ruled out by Habermas. To revert to either an
intentionalist semantics or a grounding through the phenomenological notion of intentionality
would be to return to an epistemological framework conceived within the paradigm of the
philosophy of consciousness.

[8] Ibid.

structure of linguistic communication without reference to structures of purposive activity."[9] For Culler, this strikes at the heart of speech-act theory and Habermas's interpretation or misinterpretation of it. It is impossible to eliminate purposive activity in reference to speech acts because, in Culler's words, speech-act theory "has generally worked to show that understanding utterances depends upon understanding purposive activity — what speakers are doing — and that understanding sentences is not prior to and independent of understanding sentences in action, as *linguistics* would have it, but rather dependent: *to understand sentences is to understand how they might function in purposive activity.*"[10]

Of course, when Habermas embarks upon this assault on purposive or strategic acts he has something in mind which Culler probably did not, namely Weber's diagnosis of modern culture as under the sway of *Zweckrationalität*, purposive-rational activity. Obviously, the way out would be to discover that the very form upon which Weber concentrated was in principle derivative. The problem is that linguistic communication can not be so easily separated from purposive activity. Culler's most telling point is given in an example. "To understand 'Could you close the window' is to grasp that it could be used to get someone to close the window as well as to inquire about their abilities."[11] This case makes the point that there is no state of affairs which grants to the illocutionary a certain priority and the perlocutionary a derivative status even though one might *wish* it were so.

Culler comes to a rather devastating conclusion which he repeats in various ways. "It is clear why Habermas wants to make an argument of this sort: if he cannot show that language in strategic action is somehow derivative from and dependent on language in communicative action that presupposes an ideal communicative situation, he would be left with two sorts of linguistic communication, that which presupposes these norms and that which works differently; and if he were left with two separate uses of language, appeal to the norms that subtend consensual speech situations would just be a case of choosing values that one preferred rather than relying on values inevitably implied by linguistic communication."[12] Here, Culler's perspective is limited by reference to the question of normativity.

[9] Jürgen Habermas, *The Theory of Communicative Action*, Vol. 1 (Boston, Beacon Press, 1984), p. 293.

[10] Jonathan Culler, "Communicative Competence and Normative Force," p. 137. (Emphasis mine.) Culler, who effectively criticizes the logical significance of the distinction between the perlocutionary and the illocutionary, fails in the rest of the article to come to terms with the larger framework into which Habermas places his argument. The distinction between the perlocutionary and the illocutionary, for Habermas, fits into an overall theory of rationality designed to solve the riddle of Weber's "iron cage."

[11] Ibid., p. 137.

[12] Ibid.

Yet the conclusion drawn is equally problematic for the overall attempt to correlate the project of modernity with the philosophy of language. Again, we are driven back to the question of whether or not it is possible to derive modernity's principle of emancipation from this particular reading of the philosophy of language. From Culler's point of view, "the plausibility of this argument is likely to depend in good measure on our preference for the norms of communicative action, our feeling that they are better, more basic − which is what was to be proven."[13]

(b) Between Science and Politics

If the attempt to ground the thesis about the priority of communication cannot be sustained on the basis of the use of speech-act theory we are left to question the overall status of the project as reconstructive science. Put quite simply, on what basis other than that of personal preference does the communicative thesis stand? Rolf Zimmermann's[14] penetrating critique of the Habermasian position effectively raises this question by focusing on Habermas's reconstruction of Marx's thought.

Zimmermann argues that Habermas is able to go beyond Marx by introducing a "schema of personal socialization" absent in Marx. That schema, argues Zimmermann, was present in Habermas's earlier work in the political concept of a "discussion free from domination" which "can be understood as a conversion of the political concepts of freedom and equality into a discursive-communicative schema of social mediation."[15] To this early formulation Habermas adds the concept of consensus which Zimmermann interprets as a further step in the argument, i.e., a discussion free from domination can be grounded in the concept of consensus or "true agreement." Consensus can be interpreted in a utopian or an organizational manner, the latter being preferred by Habermas. But according to Zimmermann it is impossible to strip the concept of consensus of its utopian elements. Early on, in 1962, Habermas argued that "public discussion should translate *voluntas* into *ratio* as the consensus concerning what is practically necessary in the general interest, produced in the open competition between individual arguments."[16] That concept was utopian in the

[13] Ibid.

[14] Rolf Zimmermann, *Utopie − Rationalistät − Politik. Zu Kritik, Rekonstruktion und System-atik einer emanzipatorischen Gesellschaftstheorie bei Marx und Habermas*, (Freiburg and Munich, Karl Alber 1985). In what is certainly one of the best analyses of Habermas to date, Rolf Zimmerman, a some time student of Ernst Tugendhat, distinguishes the political from the linguistic in the theory of communicative action.

[15] Rolf Zimmermann, "Emancipation and Rationality: Foundational Problems in the Theories of Marx and Habermas," in *Ratio* XXXVI: 2. (1984), p. 153.

[16] Jürgen Habermas, *Strukturwandel der Öffentlichkeit*, (Neuwied and Berlin, Luchterhand, 1962), p. 95.

sense that it assumed "freedom from all domination." Later, Habermas sought to ground this idea of consensus in "a theory of truth and language." Zimmermann, referring to Habermas's reply to Spaemann, argues that "the positive elimination of domination in terms of the conversion of voluntas into ratio assumes a normative position above the organizational principle of the discussion free from domination."

In principle, as we have seen elsewhere, Habermas attempts to eliminate utopian reference through his use and interpretation of the turn toward the analysis of language. Zimmermann observes the transition with mild irony. "For would it not in fact be a fascinating prospect, if we could show that the basic rules of language leave us no other choice, as it were, but to orientate ourselves in consensual terms and if this fact, together with our insights into the fundamental importance of an interactive schema of mediation, could demonstrate the consensual norm of emancipation to be indispensable? Or to put it more simply: What if we could show that we require nothing more than a consideration of our 'communicative competence' to support the interest in emancipation as a discursive-communicative schema?" Of course, the answer is clear: "We should witness the birth of emancipation from the spirit of language."[17]

According to Zimmermann this is precisely what Habermas does, namely, he transforms what was originally a political assumption into a transcendental or reconstructive *a priori*. Language becomes the medium for reason which discloses itself as the consensual basis for emancipation. "That is, insofar as we are rational, then we always already find ourselves in harmony with this consensual norm of emancipation."[18] From this it follows that Habermas has but to develop the social and political implications of such a theory. In other words, the principles of radical democracy are to be built into the very structure of language. Language and society are correlative. "A discursive-communicative schema of society therefore *implies* a consensual norm of emancipation, since the concept of discursive communication and understanding implies consensual rationality and its political realization requires a corresponding emancipatory principle."[19] But if that is the case, it is necessary to show more concretely the relationship between language and interaction. Hence, the Habermasian program to "project as consensual the concept of language as a general model of action for interactive behavior."[20]

From Zimmermann's perspective there are two questions regarding consensus which arise at this point: why is it necessary to arrive at things consensually and is truth a matter of consensual definition?

[17] Ibid., p. 155.
[18] Ibid.
[19] Ibid., p. 156.
[20] Ibid.

Zimmermann thinks we have "good reason to be skeptical" about this consensual approach to language. "Do we really have to combine the rather obvious step towards a radical-democratic principle of social organization, which was forced upon us by the emancipatory project developed critically in relation to Marx, with rather daring claims about consensual rationality explicated on the basis of a theory of truth and language?" In other words, Zimmermann has no problem with the utopian aspect of the Habermasian project, it is the attempt to render it, in our terms, scientific, which he questions. "Does the political dimension of the theory of emancipation so illuminatingly opened up with reference to democratic rules of mediation for society force us *nolens volens* into accepting communicative rationality as a kind of objective principle of reason?"[21] This leads to the questioning of specific aspects of the communicative theory of discursive rationality, aspects of which may be grossly overrated.

The idea of consensus, implicit in communicative rationality, can be doubted. For instance, Zimmermann argues that although the political process requires a certain kind of consensus, i.e., agreement to certain procedures, there need not be a consensus at every point. Indeed, all consensus need not be politically arrived at. "For example," Zimmermann asserts, "someone who is not demonstrably 'ideologically biased' yet argues for a greater measure of efficiency over against less interactive mediation in the name of economic or technical rationality, makes a claim to a theoretical insight which gives him [or her] a criterion of orientation for social rationality. He is not prepared to relinquish this because he simply believes his theoretical assertions to be 'true.'"[22] The example makes a point, namely, that all truth is not consensually, that is to say politically, derived. Hence, to follow the argument, "we can draw a distinction between a *political concept* of discursive rationality in the sense of radical-democratic social mediation and a concept of discursivity based upon truth as a criterion."[23] Hence, the criterion of discursivity essential to the thesis with regard to the primacy of communication "proves to be too weak as a criterion of truth."[24] This in turn leads to a series of problems with the concept of communicative action. Following Zimmermann's argument as reformulated from Ernst Tugendhat, one can and perhaps should differentiate between the nature of language and the nature of communication. This distinction, of course, leads to a denial of the isomorphism between the external structure of linguistic communication and the internal structure of language which Karl-Otto Apel perceived to be evolving, upon which Habermas builds his

[21] Ibid., p. 157.
[22] Ibid., p. 160.
[23] Ibid.
[24] Ibid.

case.[25] It follows from the dissolution of this isomorphism so essential to the claims of communicative action, that discursive procedures do not necessarily eliminate conflicting truth claims of justification in terms of verification; the point being that all claims for truth are not discursively arrived at even if certain procedures are followed. Presumably, there is a difference between discoursing about the nature of things and arriving at the truth about the nature of things. In other words, the nature of theoretical truth is not necessarily found in discourse while the nature of practical truth is in discourse but not in discursive consensus.

The point of Zimmermann's analysis is to strike a blow at Habermas's attempt to read the principle of consensus out of the nature of language. If the political program of consensus with its implied assumptions about emancipation is not isomorphic with the nature of discursive interaction, then the program Habermas is pursuing is indeed based upon utopian principles. Although, as I shall show later, this conclusion leads to serious problems with the theory of communicative action, Zimmermann has no difficulty with it. In fact, he finds the real contribution of Habermas to be in the realm of the construction of a political ethics. What is unique about the Habermasian program is his connection of "the radical-democratic program of emancipation and his political-communicative ethics" with "a sociological interpretation of modern society which turns the interactive-communicative principle of socialization into a kind of socio-structural necessity."[26] This correlates with Habermas's takeover of the positive elements in Weber and Durkheim's theories which require, as a consequence of the dissolution of traditional modes of social integration, "an imperative need for what we may call post-traditional social integration." Human beings must take over the social organization of their world themselves and this can only become "a real social possibility through communicative forms of mediation. In this fashion communicative action takes over the function of social coordination and integration."[27]

---

[25] This is the key assumption upon which a consensus theory of language is built. Tugendhat and Zimmermann show that the scientific evidence for this argument is at best difficult to render. Habermas and Apel are building on an idealization of the pragmatism or pragmaticism of Charles Sanders Peirce. As Peirce assumed a future consensus regarding scientific inquiry, so Apel and Habermas assume that this insight can be applied to the nature of language. Hence, language conceived as communication presupposes consensus. But this assumption can be questioned. Tugendhat and Zimmermann argue that in the case of theoretical truth consensus need not be assumed. Galileo's theoretical observations about the universe were correct, even though there was no reigning consensus. Further, they argue that although practical truth is discursively arrived at, it does not necessarily presuppose consensus. The assumption here is that political action does not presuppose universal agreement.

[26] Ibid., p. 161.

[27] Ibid., p. 162.

Indeed, what Zimmermann, by implication, suggests is that the debate turn to the question of the grounding of an ethics, a suggestion which has in fact become a reality in the post-1982 period of Habermas's writing. However, if one takes the very precise criticism of Culler regarding speech-act theory, with the more general criticism of Zimmermann regarding the the failure of language theory to secure one against the potentialities of utopian thought, a potential flaw in the theory of communicative action begins to be revealed which no amount of reconstructive "scientific" argument can cover up.

One might pause for a moment to reflect on the point of departure for the construction of a theory of communicative action. The question comes to this: how successful is the program for reconstructive science which Habermas constructs? If the arguments for the distinction between the illocutionary and the perlocutionary do not stand, if the claims for the communicative resolution of questions of truth and validity are not sustainable, just how valid is this turn toward reconstructive science?

II   The System/Lifeworld Distinction

As the foundation of the theory of language is the primacy of the communicative over the strategic, so the end of social theory is liberation from the consequences of strategic action in the form of the colonization of the lifeworld. When strategic action is primary, the critical thesis is that ordinary, normal forms of discursive interaction are distorted. When systems imperatives superimpose themselves over lifeworld imperatives, a distortion of the lifeworld occurs. Although closer to the instrumental and strategic than the communicative, Habermas incorporates the insights of systems theory in his construction of a theory of society. Certainly, the ideal of an open, communicative, emancipatory society based, in contrast to utopian claims, on the firm foundation of reconstructive science is appealing not only as a way of justifying language claims but as a theory of society as well. However, if the above-mentioned criticisms give the clue to what the critics have found to be the flaw in Habermas's more recent development, namely, the attempt, in the name of reconstructive science, to establish as legitimate, principles which would otherwise be derived from political argument and interpretation, the system/lifeworld distinction, with its reliance on systems theory, fares little better than did the earlier foray into speech-act theory.

(a)   The Questionable Contribution of Systems Theory

Thomas McCarthy's complex and interesting criticism of the system/lifeworld distinction[28] as it exists in the second volume of *The Theory of Communicative Action*, sustains similar doubts about the nature of what we have called reconstructive science as it applies to systems theory. McCarthy concludes his essay on "Complexity and Democracy, or The Seducements of Systems Theory" with this trenchant comment: "Habermas once criticized Marx for succumbing to the illusion of rigorous science, and he traced a number of Marxism's historical problems with political analysis and political practice to this source. The question I have wanted to pose here is whether in flirting with systems theory he does not run the danger of being seduced by the same illusion in more modern dress."[29]

Habermas, since the publication of *Legitimation Crisis*, has wanted to use the distinction between system and lifeworld as a way of reduplicating, under the paradigm of communication, what Marx presented in a now almost universally acknowledged flawed manner, i.e., the distinction between base and superstructure. The great advantage of Marx's distinction between base and superstructure is that it enabled him to grasp dimensions of social analysis that were not immediately apparent to consciousness. Hence the turn from consciousness to an analysis of material conditions, as evidenced in *The German Ideology*, represented in Marx's own view that transition which would enable his "scientific" analysis to achieve a comprehensive understanding of the contradictions of society unavailable to his more naive colleagues. As is well known, out of this distinction between things as they appear to consciousness and things as they "really are," Marx was able to make his famous diagnosis of society under the category of "fetishism." The great problem for later Marxist analysis has been to keep alive the intention of this insight without succumbing to its particular limitations. Hence, the path – from fetishism to reification to instrumental reason.

Habermas's own attempt is to use the distinction between system and lifeworld as a way of sustaining the concept of reification under the rubric, "inner colonization of the lifeworld." The concept is intentionally complex, involving another aspect of Habermas's view of modernity and modernization. The theory, developed through a reworking of Mead, Durkheim and Parsons, perceives modernization as the progressive de-coupling of the originally integrated system and lifeworld. The issue becomes one of understanding how system and lifeworld interface with one another.

The great problem in Habermas's view is that the modern subsystems of

[28] The system/lifeworld distinction builds upon the communicative thesis in the sense that the forms of the lifeworld are rendered ideally as communicative. However, even though derived from a form of instrumental reason, the so-called scientific insights of systems theory are said to contribute to an overall theory of society.

[29] *New German Critique*, 35 (Spring/Summer, 1985), p. 53.

economy and state which reproduce themselves materially, interfere in the process of the symbolic reproduction of daily life. They act functionally. This means that the processes of mediation between system and lifeworld are perceived under imperatives of money and power in functional terms exclusive of communicative interaction. Hence, exclusive of means of communicative interaction, the symbolic reproduction of the lifeworld occurs in functional terms under the rubrics of money and power. It is precisely here, according to Habermas, that the term "internal colonization of the lifeworld" occurs.[30]

In a manner which parallels the argument of Zimmermann, in the sense that it critiques the latent scientism of Habermas's mode of argumentation, McCarthy argues that Habermas, contrary to his earlier critiques of systems theory, has been more recently seduced by it, perhaps for reasons of the supposed scientific accuracy as indicated in the quote above. In other words, the turn towards systems theory would represent for Habermas a turn away form the "utopian" dangers involved in direct political analysis, and a turn toward establishing analysis on the firm foundations of science. McCarthy argues that if this is not the wrong turn it is at least a confusing and ambiguous one in Habermas's thought, particularly when conceived against the backdrop of his earlier arguments against systems theory. In effect, this amounts to eliminating from analysis the "utopian content" of "our political tradition." The question then becomes one of whether imperatives are systemically or socially integrated. McCarthy argues that the choice is not simply one between systemic and social integration, but rather one in which they, "as they are defined by Habermas, seem to be extremes rather than alternatives that exhaust the field of possibilities: the denial of one does not entail the other."[31] McCarthy fears that by relying on systems theory Habermas undermines the essentially utopian content of his own political analysis, a utopian content which "must remain the regulative idea" for "critical social theory." Put simply, cashing in on the so-called scientific benefits of systems theory occurs at the price of rendering a participatory political system obsolete. Yet that very political possibility must remain the motivating basis for a theory of communicative action.

McCarthy asserts that Habermas "takes over so much of the conceptual arsenal of systems theory that he runs the risk of not being able to formulate in these terms an answer"[32] to the question of the place of the forms of representative democracy in his system. Indeed, it is McCarthy's

---

[30] Ideally, the system/lifeworld distinction, along with the critical thesis that is its result, the internal colonization of the lifeworld, would enable a critique parallel to Marx's theory of fetishism and Lukács's theory of reification without the flaws of either.

[31] Ibid., p. 41.

[32] Ibid., p. 43.

argument that Habermas takes over so much of systems theory because of its seeming "theoretical" virtue. But, asks McCarthy, does systems theory really present us with an advance? While it has "made sense to approach biological systems as unified, integrated, adapted systems which have been naturally selected" it is not necessarily the same with respect to "social systems." "Is biocybernetics going to be any more fruitful a model of society than classical mechanics was? It has some of the same drawbacks, for instance the traditional ideological twist of treating what is social, and thus potentially the object of human will, as natural, and thus purely a matter of objectified relations, objects and events." McCarthy goes on to coin a somewhat ironic metaphor, "Habermas hopes to dissolve this solidity in the waters of systems theory." And then the warning: "But it may just prove to be insoluble."[33] He agrees with Habermas to the extent that "*some* type of functional analysis is essential to the reconstruction of the Marxian project. The question is, what type of functional analysis?"[34]

In the end, McCarthy takes a highly critical view of the place of systems theory in Habermas's later work. "We do not need the paraphernalia of social systems theory to identify unintended consequences." Instead he proposes a kind of functional analysis more in line with Habermas's earlier work. "This notion of a theoretically generalized narrative, drawing upon both hermeneutical and functional modes of analysis, was the developed form of Habermas's long-standing idea of a historically oriented theory of society with a practical intent."[35] According to McCarthy, the great advantage of this approach is that "it retained an intrinsic relation to practice: guided by an emancipatory interest, social analysis was undertaken from the standpoint of realizing, to the extent possible at a given stage of development, a form of organization based on unrestricted and undistorted communication. The truth of such analysis could be finally confirmed only through the successful continuation of our *Bildungsprozesse*."[36]

McCarthy concludes with the not too subtle suggestion that the paradigm for the transition from the earlier to the later Habermas is to be found in transition from the early to the later Marx which, as the youthful Habermas so brilliantly pointed out, eliminated *praxis* in the name of positive science. This is not to say that Habermas has succumbed to the dilemmas of positivism, but it does suggest that the temptation to rest the case on the surely contested, but none the less seemingly secure, foundations of a form of reconstructive science is difficult to resist.

[33] Ibid., p. 49.
[34] Ibid., p. 50.
[35] Ibid., p. 53.
[36] Ibid.

(b)   Hermeneutics vs Systems Theory

While McCarthy questions the validity of systems theory, Dieter Misgeld[37] takes the argument a step further by attempting to eliminate the distinction between system and lifeworld altogether. Misgeld understands the earlier claims of critical theory as distinguished from mainline sociological theory to be that it is "practically enlightening," while the intention of mainline sociological theory is that it be theoretically cogent. Misgeld suggests that with the publication of *The Theory of Communicative Action* Habermas, in effect, gives up on critical theory and joins with what amounts to normal sociology. "Thus, the neo-functionalist sociological theorist Jeffrey C. Alexander treats TCA as a work belonging to the tradition of Parsonian theory. When he refers to Habermas's 'critical Parsonianism' he can easily reduce the meaning of 'critical' in this phrase to Habermas's diagnosis of a conflict, in late capitalist societies, between 'lifeworlds' — worlds of experience and symbolic discourse — and system or structure."[38] Misgeld concludes that "The differences between Parsons and Habermas reduce to the difference between a highly general explanatory sociological theory (Parsons) and a social theory which is philosophically illuminating."[39] Misgeld's claim is simply that Habermas's incorporation of systems theory eliminates a critical theory of society because it cuts the Gordian knot between theory and practice. In other words, the distinction between "system" and "lifeworld" is misleading because "it detracts from the practical point of the theory and blocks reflection upon actual social situations in the relevant societies of our times."[40] Not only that, argues Misgeld, but the distinction also gives the priority in terms of analysis to the system over the lifeworld. "Societies in general, i.e., general mechanisms for their mainten- ance and self-differentiation, can only be analyzed at the level of systems- theoretical abstractions. The concrete historical lifeworlds of particular societies cannot serve as a starting point for reflection on social develop- ment." Therefore, "Habermas subordinates the lifeworld approach to sys- tems-theoretical arguments. In this case, the explanations sought after are not motivated by practical questions. Their point is to give objective know- ledge of the society, or even of social reproduction in general, independently from any consideration of how this knowledge can orient our actions always taking place within particular societies."[40] Misgeld acknowledges that there

---

[37] I find Misgeld's analysis, informed as it is by Gadamer, interesting because it highlights the critique of systems theory that can be made from a hermeneutic perspective.

[38] Dieter Misgeld, "Critical Hermeneutics vs NeoParsonianism," *New German Critique*, 35 (Spring/Summer, 1985), p. 56.

[39] Ibid., p. 59.

[40] Ibid., p. 60.

is indeed a second conception of the relation between system and lifeworld which "is primarily practical and critical. It asks whether the present state of conflict between formally rationalized systems of action, such as the economy, public administration ('bureaucracy'), and practical orientation dependent on communication can be overcome."[41] In order to sustain this second view, Misgeld would dissolve the system back into the lifeworld which, he argues, one cannot get out of anyway. "I am suggesting ... that knowledge of society in the final analysis always is knowledge gained *in* the lifeworld."[42] It follows that if critical knowledge were always available within the lifeworld, instead of appearing at the interface between system and lifeworld, one could also eliminate the need for a theory of evolution. In fact, Misgeld argues, the theory of evolution actually prevents the development of critical knowledge. "When raising questions about this program by criticizing its propensity toward systems theoretical argument-ation, I am merely pointing out that actual achievements of practical *and* socially critical knowledge *in* society are neglected." Do we really need a theory of evolution "in order to defend a normative *and* tentatively held commitment to social emancipation from experienced forms of defeat, humiliation and extreme impoverishment and renunciation?"[43] Instead, Misgeld claims that "emancipation is a practical-moral concept belonging within the context of the reasoning we do about the society all the time while living in it. It cannot be made stronger by way of a theory which puts the society before us in its entirety."[44] And if society cannot be theorized in the manner in which Habermas wishes, Misgeld questions Habermas's advance of the overall project of critical theory:

It is doubtful that giving critical theory a rigorous form, as Habermas attempts to do, amounts to a great advance over the evocative force of, let us say, "The Dialectic of Enlightenment." While this work may have been methodologically naive from Habermas's perspective and certainly subject to the deceptions Habermas criticizes, it at least had the force of an immediate, direct response to historical experience. While it presented itself as objective theory, it can be read as an imaginative, frequently startling narrative interpretation of the fate of modernity which provokes more questions, so to speak, than a theory can achieve which relies on procedures for the systematic objectification of social experience and then has to find methods for the translation of its findings back into the world of acting and communicating societal members.[45]

[41] Ibid., p. 63.
[42] Ibid.
[43] Ibid., p. 69.
[44] Ibid.
[45] Ibid., p. 80.

Misgeld's biting critique, which places the theory of communicative action behind the *Dialectic of Enlightenment*, may be unfair. After all, it is apparent that most hermeneutic analysis by itself is often a-critical. In fact, hermeneutic analysis has often been used to legitimate pre-enlightenment traditions. Misgeld is thus forced to show why analyses anchored in the lifeworld are automatically critical. However, systems-theoretical statements, as both Misgeld and McCarthy point out, are not automatically legitimate, and certainly they do not render a form of theoretical analysis scientific, thereby securing it from the limitations of those forms of analysis that are anchored in *praxis*.

(c) The System/Lifeworld Distinction in the Context of Power

A third reading of Habermas makes an even more penetrating criticism of the distinction between system and lifeworld. Axel Honneth, in an excellent study of the notion of power in French and German thought, *Kritique der Macht*,[46] makes the point that the distinction between system and lifeworld functions as a kind of dualism which enables communication to be separated from power. Ultimately, the distinction is based upon two theoretical fictions, namely, that an action system can occur independently of the normative building of consensus, and that a communicatively integrated action sphere, the lifeworld, can occur independently of domination by relations of power.

This kind of criticism gets at the heart of both the critical and constructive elements of the theory of communicative action. In the context of the pre-history of critical theory, Habermas wants to overcome the pessimism of his predecessors by locating a sphere where reason and rationalization occur uncorrupted by relations of domination. In a sense, by so doing it would be possible to overcome the charge of *Dialectic of Enlightenment* which was that domination and enlightenment occur simultaneously. In French thought, Foucault extended this analysis with historical precision by showing that with the onslaught of the so-called historical enlightenment the institutions of oppression became ever more dominant. Hence, in the modern period, the handmaiden of reason was power.

In recent years Habermas has wanted to counter that thesis by at least two strategies. The first has been to locate within language the priority of the communicative over the strategic. The second has been an attempt to secure the realm of the lifeworld from invasions from contemporary forms of domination. This is not to suggest that the lifeworld actually exists free from the imperatives of a strategic rationality, but that it can be perceived at least theoretically as a realm sheltered from external invasions by other

---

[46] *Kritik der Macht* (Frankfurt am Main: Suhrkamp, 1985).

media. The result is the ability to make a distinction between a normal and a pathological view of the lifeworld. In the normal view, the spheres of culture, society, and personality, the matrix of human social interaction, would be transferred from one generation to another without interference. Actually, this process is obstructed at all times by mechanisms seeking to subvert this seemingly normal process. Hence, Habermas derives a pathology from the distinction between system and lifeworld. In the simplest terms, when the normal process is interfered with we have what could be called the colonization of the lifeworld. In more complex terms, Habermas claims that when the media of money and power, the imperatives of the social system, take over the lifeworld and recast structures that were accessible communicatively in instrumental and strategic forms, it becomes colonized. But this is true if, and only if, it is possible to separate system from social imperatives; if, in Honneth's terms, one is able both to sustain the dualism between system and lifeworld and to idealize the lifeworld in such a way that it is separated from power.

What is crucial for this dualistic understanding of the distinction between system and lifeworld is the differentiation between material and symbolic reproduction. Following a distinction made early on between labor and interaction, Habermas has developed the view that an actual distinction can be sustained between the two ways society in the general sense can reproduce itself. As students of Hegel well know, in the Jena *Philosophy of Mind*, Hegel made a dialectical distinction between, in Habermas's terms, "symbolic representation, the labor process, and interaction on the basis of reciprocity."[47] In that essay, Habermas radicalizes Hegel's famous thesis in the following manner: "It is not the spirit in the absolute movement of reflecting on itself which manifests itself in, among other things, language, labor and moral relationships, but rather, it is the dialectical interconnections between linguistic symbolization, labor and interaction which determine the concept of spirit."[48] In other words, the great task, the dialectical heritage from Hegel and Marx on, is to capture the proper relationship between labor on the one hand and language on the other. But that is "tricky" precisely because of the history of interpretation which can tilt the relationship in either an idealistic or a materialistic way. If one were to idealize this relationship, labor would be subsumed under the category of language in such a manner that the instrumental framework of the larger social system would remain unmasked. The relationship can become equally problematic if one considers it from the opposite perspective, which would serve to unmask the categories of the social system.

---

[47] Jürgen Habermas, "Labor and Interaction: Remarks on Hegel's Jena *Philosophy of Mind*," in *Theory and Practice* (Boston, Beacon Press, 1973), pp. 142–69.
[48] Ibid., p. 143.

This gives the clue to the way Habermas has read and continues to read Marx. Habermas thinks that as the tool is the mediator between subject and object in Hegel of the Jena period, so for Marx, "instrumental action" interpreted as "the productive activity which regulates the material interchange of the human species with its natural environment" becomes the paradigm for "production." We should note carefully here that production in this interpretation is the equivalent of instrumental action. And, according to Habermas, from this is to be derived the paradigmatic fall from grace of either Marx or his interpreters or perhaps both. "Because of this, Marx's brilliant insight into the dialectical relationship between the forces of production and the relations of production could very quickly be misinterpreted in a mechanistic manner."[49]

Habermas's comment is instructive. If anything, he has attempted to sustain the distinction between labor and interaction. "Today, when the attempt is being undertaken to reorganize the communicative nexus of interactions, no matter how much they have hardened into quasi-natural forms, according to the model of technically progressive systems of rational goal-directed action, *we have reason enough to keep these two dimensions more rigorously separated.*"[50] He goes on to reflect about the necessary difference between the "technical forces of production" and "the development of norms which could fulfill the dialectic of moral relationships in an interaction free of domination."[51]

Finally, the essay ends with this most declarative statement over which interpreters of Habermas might forever puzzle: "*Liberation from hunger and misery* does not necessarily converge with *liberation from servitude and degradation*, for there is no automatic developmental relation between labor and interaction."[52] Indeed, if the relationship is not automatic the task remains to specify it, if for no other reason than "there is a connection between the two dimensions." This relationship, which two decades later became the relationship between system and lifeworld, is even then seen as having imperative significance. "Neither the Jena *Realphilosophie* nor *The German Ideology* have clarified it adequately, but in any case they can persuade us of its relevance: the self-formative process of spirit as well as of our species essentially depends on that relation between labor and interaction."[53]

Honneth suggests that this more recent formulation of the distinction between system and lifeworld sustains two theoretical fictions, namely that

[49] Ibid., p. 169.
[50] Ibid. (Emphasis mine.)
[51] Ibid.
[52] Ibid.
[53] Ibid.

certain social systems are constructed independently of processes of consensus, while the lifeworld can be conceived independently of power and domination. It is indeed ironic, as Honneth points out, that this very theoretical analysis insulates the social system from criticism while isolating the lifeworld from praxeological orientation. No more penetrating criticism could be made of one whose earlier work seemed to be grounded in *praxis*. What is even worse, from our point of view, is that the very attempt to ground the theory in the rigors of reconstructive science robs it of its utopian force.

Conclusion

From a brief look at some of the more significant criticism of Habermas's work one can conclude that not only is the emancipatory thesis, as located in a reconstruction of the philosophy of language, uncertain, but that the very attempt to locate critique in the distinction between system and lifeworld undermines the rather insecure status claimed for emancipation. Hence, it appears that the overall status of the Habermasian enterprise is at dual purposes. If we were to take the larger project in its best sense it would appear that the attempt to secure the primacy of communication in the philosophy of language is undercut by the distinction between system and lifeworld — because that distinction restricts major areas of human social experience from formation through processes based on communication. Yet that restriction, as indicated by the concept of system and material reproduction, conflicts with the idea that all linguistic phenomena have their originary form in communication, precisely because in terms of the social system only some phenomena can be classified under the rubric of consensus. Hence, the argument which supports the linguistic turn toward social theory, and the argument which supports the distinction between system and lifeworld, are at odds with one another. The desire to secure the primacy of the emancipatory in the former context (language) is undermined by the attempt to restrict the emancipatory in the latter (society).

A brief look at the criticism suggests that there are further problems. On the one hand, it has not been clearly demonstrated that the assumption regarding language concerning the primacy of communicative over strategic forms of discourse has been established. Hence, the attempt to ground the theory of communicative action in a theory of language remains unclear and is certainly not established by the claims of a reconstructive science. At best, the communicative thesis is grounded in a utopian assumption about the way society ought to be. At the same time, the distinction between system and lifeworld tends to rob even that thesis of its force, inasmuch as the utopian insight upon which critique rests is lost in the supposed scienticism of a biocybernetic insight regarding the primacy of ideas derived from systems theory. Hence, the project of modernity which is supposed to show how the emancipatory thesis, the brainchild of the enlightenment, can be sustained through an analysis of the progressive differentiation between system and lifeworld under the paradigm of the transition to the philosophy of language, resolves itself in a series of contradictions which echo the beliefs of their author but remain in the insecure world of desire.

4

Discourse Ethics

I Universalism vs Communitarianism in Ethics

In the context of Habermas's later works, the theory of communicative action provides the basis for forays into other areas. Certainly the foremost of these is the one leading into ethics. This development should not be surprising. At the very top of the agenda of German enlightenment thought was the attempt to somehow establish a basis for ethics that fully acknowledged that the traditional world had disappeared. Both Kant and Hegel represent versions of this realization, though Hegel subsequently attempted to undermine Kant by turning to a modern form of *Sittlichkeit* to ground his view of ethics. Kant's attempt to build a theory of ethics on the basis of a notion of rationality alone has the abstract advantage of avoiding recourse to cultural traditions for ethical grounding. Hegel chose the option Kant rejected; using the philosophy of history as a kind of dramatic forum where virtue (*Tugend*) would ultimately be overcome by the way of the world (*Weltlauf*).[1] His critique of Kant presumed that one could show concretely what Kant assumed could only be demonstrated abstractly on the basis of a certain view of rationality, namely, that embedded within the emerging structures of culture one finds new and better forms of ethical interaction which in one way or another overcome the limits of the past.

Kant and Hegel represent two different approaches to modernity, one of which attempts to approach the ethical dilemmas of modernity in terms of the rigorous demands of modern rationality, while the other views rationality as embedded within emerging cultural and historical forms. In one way or another, these two versions of the German enlightenment provide the forum for the vigorous, heated, and in many ways exciting contemporary debate in ethics. Kant, already anticipating the ethical relativism of Locke's dualistic solution to the problem of ethics, attempted to ground ethics in

[1] I refer to the section of Hegel's *Phenomenology*, where the way of the world (modernity), seen through the development of political economy and modern politics, triumphs over the classical notion of virtue. G.W.F Hegel, *The Phenomenology of Spirit*, tr. A.V. Miller (Oxford, Oxford University Press, 1977), pp. 228–35.

the forms of rationality alone. Hegel, endeavoring to go beyond a simple repetition of the principle of non-contradiction, found Kant's approach to be based not only on a simple abstraction, but also dissociated from forms of life as represented in modern history and culture. The universalists and the communitarians find their respective forebearers in the German enlightenment, even though explicit reference is not always made. The Hegelian charge of abstraction is made by those who would wish to anchor a view of ethics in specific forms of life;[2] while the charge made by the universalists is that a principle beyond specific reference to a particular culture is necessary in order to avoid the potential pitfalls implicit in the allegiance to a particular culture or tradition.

How to construct an ethics that will not succumb to the distortions of a potentially destructive cultural tradition? That is the question, the Habermasian question, which, although it cannot be answered directly, must occupy the center of any ethical position. One is tempted to turn to biography. For Habermas, born into a world which was shaped by National Socialism, the dilemma of a Hegelian solution is clear: an ethic based on the forms of life existing within a culture, would, and in fact did, legitimate acts which we know to be the very contradiction of ethical behavior. So the problem becomes one of finding a way to anchor an ethics in the dilemmas of modernity while at the same time avoiding the potentially destructive influence of essentially corrupt and distorted cultural traditions.[3] The solution: discourse or communicative ethics. Discourse ethics links basic insights regarding the philosophy of language (discourse) with a certain analysis of modernity. Generally, discourse ethics is interpreted as the triumph of the Kantian influence.[4] To be sure, one finds here echoes of the Kantian attempt to ground an ethics in the nature of an argument. Indeed, the idea of the good is, as in Kant, replaced by the notion of the good will. And the general assumption implicit in the tripartite division of modernity into truth, normativity, and expressivity, which was more or less put forth by Kant, is granted a further grounding by Habermas.

If Hegel is dismissed, he is not totally abandoned. Whereas Hegel attempted to justify his interpretation of modernity in terms of a philosophy

---

[2] In the strict sense, Hegel is not a communitarian. While he grounds an ethic in the emerging values of a community, he supports the necessary emergence of the concrete universal. Hence, in the *Philosophy of Right*, the universalism of "abstract right" eventually conforms to the ethical communitarian forms of family, civil society and, most importantly from Hegel's point of view, the state. Modern communitarians would most likely find themselves at odds with this element of the Hegelian program.

[3] This problem will re-emerge in the contest of my discussion of Habermas's philosophy of law. It is certainly one major source of Habermas's anti-contextualism.

[4] In the more recent publications Habermas has moved ever closer to Kant.

of history, representing the simultaneous evolution of reason and subjectivity, Habermas replaces the philosophy of history with the notion of reconstructive science. Hence, the discourse ethic is complemented by the reconstruction of the modern subject *vis-à-vis* the quasi-scientific investigations of Lawrence Kohlberg. Kohlberg's theory of moral development provides the justification for talking about what Habermas calls a "post-conventional" morality whose fundamental character will be designated as reciprocity, and which can be considered truly universal. In this sense, morality as a universal structure transcending particular cultures both transcends and is indigenous to forms of existence characterizing ethical life (*Sittlichkeit*). Hegel is incorporated and transcended both by recourse to a Kantian form of argumentation and by appeal to the insights of a so-called reconstructive science. Implicit here is a distinction made (as Habermas once quipped, made only in Frankfurt) between morality (*Moralität*) and ethics (*Sittlichkeit*).[5]

The distinction seems to support well the problem referred to a moment ago. If one relies simply on forms of life embedded in particular cultures to justify progressive modes of enlightenment, i.e., the course of human freedom, one finds oneself in the peculiar situation of being without standards with which to criticize those very forms when they are corrupted. The appeal to *Moralität* enables one to cite forms of universality which transcend particular cultures.[6] From this point of view, neo-Aristotelian thought is always in the bind of particularity, unable to develop standards for critique of those very life forms which exist within a particular culture. Hence, appeal to a universalism represented both in the structure of argumentation and complemented by universal insights taken from the developments of reconstructive science (the theory of moral development) overcomes the dilemmas of an ethics based on cultural analysis alone.

II Peirce and the Ideal Community of Speech

In a sense, the original idea for a discourse ethics comes from Charles Sanders Peirce as reinterpreted through the semantic idealism of Karl-Otto Apel.[7] Peirce's idea was that the possibility of scientific truth presupposed a scientific community which could make judgments on the validity

[5] This distinction reflects a similar distinction made by Hegel in his *Philosophy of Right*, tr. T. M. Knox, (Oxford, Oxford University Press, 1942).

[6] Hence, the appeal to morality enables Habermas to overcome what he considers to be the contextualist dilemma.

[7] Karl-Otto Apel, *Charles S. Peirce. From Pragmatism to Pragmaticism*, tr. John Michail Krois (Amherst, University of Massachusetts Press, 1981).

or invalidity of scientific achievements. The quest for scientific truth, therefore, could be found in the decision to seek the truth, which in principle requires a normative decision preceding the discovery of scientific truth, the locus of which is to be found in the ideally postulated scientific community. As Apel would point out later, the very procedure of science requires as its precedent certain normative assumptions regarding the nature of scientific inquiry.[8] The Kantian implications of this reconstruction of the nature of scientific inquiry would not be lost. Peirce could be interpreted as one who, when referring to a particular inquiry, like Kant, could be seen to depart from a purely empirical investigation to raise the question of the transcendental conditions for the possibility of such an investigation. But, unlike Kant, Peirce located those conditions not in the intuitions of an investigating subject, but in the postulation of an ideal community of investigators whose mutual understanding would regulate the nature of scientific truth.

It is clear that Peirce's insight is significant not only for the development of a discourse ethics, but that it was fundamental to the theory of communicative action itself. However, what interests me in this reference to Peirce is the normative character of the reference to a communal adjudication of determinations regarding the nature of validity. Peirce's shift of reference from the nature of things to the nature of communities and the discourses they use would change the nature of reflection on ethics. Habermas, along with Apel, has, of course, moved beyond Peirce, but in a peculiar way discourse ethics is an elaboration of his basic insight. The idea that validity is somehow determined communally finds its elaboration at the base of a discourse ethic. What is significant about Habermas's approach to the creation of an ethic is that he explores the nature of the formation of normative categories at a level of pure abstraction, considering the conditions for the possibility of agreement on normative claims, independent of any material or historical determination. This, of course, is an idealization. But it has the advantage, or so some would say, of freeing ethical reflection from institutional representation, a problem as old as Plato's *Republic*.[9]

If Peirce provides the communal idealization necessary for the construction of a discourse ethic, one can return to Kant to provide the basis for its

[8] This insight supports Habermas's normative reading of modernity. Given the Peircian insight into the normative presuppositions of scientific inquiry, vast areas of investigation fall under the canopy of normativity.

[9] The problem as it occurs in Plato's *Republic* is reflected in the attempt to find an historical example on which to base the discussion of justice. Eventually, all historically existing prototypes are rejected. Socrates is then forced to construct an ideal, imaginary *polis* in which justice can be found.

central motif, namely, the procedure of universalization. Here, Habermas
attempts to reconstruct the conditions of the categorical imperative at the
level of speech as a way of grounding the very limited claims of moral
theory.[10] At its heart, moral theory articulates the discursive procedures
implicit in processes of universalization[11] which characterize argumentation.
The claims of the discourse ethic at this level are minimal, but central.
Habermas makes a distinction between norms and values.[12] Whereas a
discourse ethic can outline the procedures by which norms are established,
it lays no claims to the articulation of particular values, or so it would seem.
In turn, the procedures can be established in two ways: first, through an
analysis of the structures of argumentation, the philosophy of language
part; second, through a complementary inquiry into the development of
moral psychology.[13]

III   Toward a Procedural Ethic

If the proper domain of ethics is the determination of a realm where right
can be distinguished from wrong,[14] the task of ethical reflection will be to
account for determining the procedures for normative validity. For Habermas, this is essentially a cognitive[15] task. The mere fact that a particular
norm could be accepted by a community as valid does not establish its
validity as such.[16] Consequently, it is necessary to turn to the inner logic of
moral argumentation to determine the validity or the invalidity of a norm.[17]
This assumption allows Habermas to introduce the principle of universalization.[18] It is precisely through the introduction of the principle of univer-

[10] Jürgen Habermas, *Moralbewusstsein und kommunikatives Handeln* (Frankfurt am Main,
Suhrkamp, 1983), pp. 73–4, 88–9.

[11] Ibid., pp. 74–8, 103.

[12] This distinction would apply to the critique of communitarianism. Communitarianism
would begin at the level of values.

[13] Ibid., 127–200. See also, "Die philosophischen Grundannahmen der Kohlbergschen
Theorie," pp. 130–43.

[14] Ibid., pp. 55, 59–60. The question "What should I do?" determines the sphere of moral
inquiry.

[15] Ibid., pp. 53–4. Habermas identifies discourse ethics with the tradition of cognitive
ethics developed with Kant.

[16] Obviously, this is a point against communitarians. For example, the fact that South
Africa endorses apartheid as a norm does not establish its validity. A communitarianism which
eschews universalism will probably have difficulty at this point.

[17] In Habermas's view, the determination of validity begins with the differentiation of
normative from descriptive statements. Ibid., pp. 60–7.

[18] Ibid., p. 75. Habermas attempts to reconstruct Kant's "Categorical Imperative" as an
intersubjectively valid norm. As such, the form of universalization implicit in the establishment

salization that a rational consensus can be achieved in the context of a multitude of opinions which may conflict. The cognitivist principle involved here is that a norm is right when it corresponds to a general or generalizable interest. So conceived, the interest of any individual can be accepted by all those involved.

In turn, we are then led to a consideration of the presuppositions of discourse. No one should be excluded. Everybody should be given a right to make his or her own claims and to criticize others. The only norms valid are those regulating common interests.[19] In other words, normative validity is determined by acceptance of the principle of universalization. Universalization, the basic principle of a discourse ethic, implies a specific procedure whereby contested norms are accepted once their consequences are understood by all without coercion. One might claim that it is this principle which every ethic attempts to develop.

Acceptance of the principle of universalization allows one to turn to a procedure for determining the validity of norms. They are valid when, in the context of practical discourse, they are determined by rational consensus.[20] In Habermas's view, this argument provides a grounding of an ethics but not a final one, a *Letzbegrundung*, as Apel argued following Kant's attempt to find an *a priori* valid moral principle. In other words, the argument offered by Habermas is open to empirical falsification.[21] Equally,

of norms is intersubjective. Hence, the principles of communicative action are developed at the level of universalization. Universalization of norms will follow the rules of practical agreement.

[19] These three principles, the right of making claims and criticizing others, the principle of inclusion, and the limitation of norms to the sphere of common interest form the basis of the argument for universalization. As such it is a procedural argument.

[20] Habermas in the discourse ethic is building on his consensus theory of truth and validity initially outlined in his "What Is Universal Pragmatics?". "The goal of coming to an understanding (*Verständigung*) is to bring about an agreement (*Einverständnis*) that terminates in the intersubjective mutuality of reciprocal understanding and shared knowledge, mutual trust, and accord with one another. Agreement is based on recognition of corresponding validity claims of comprehensibility, truth, truthfulness, and rightness. We can see the word *understanding* is ambiguous. In its minimal meaning, it indicates that two subjects understand a linguistic expression in the same way; its maximal meaning is that between the two there exists an accord containing the rightness of an utterance in relation to a mutually recognized normative background. In addition, two participants in communication can come to an understanding about something in the world, and they can make their intentions understandable to one another." Jürgen Habermas, *Communication and the Evolution of Society*, tr. T. McCarthy (Boston, Beacon Press, 1979), p. 3.

[21] Habermas wants to maintain that his discourse ethics is open to falsification by scientific evidence. New scientific evidence then could render the findings of discourse ethics invalid. But does this mean that the discourse ethics is purely empirical?

the ethics may be characterized as a formal ethic, in the sense that it offers no substantive ethical orientation. Therefore it does not provide a basis for adjudication between alternative value systems.[22] This means that a differentiation has been made between questions of justice, which are derived from universalistic procedures, and questions of the good life, which are posed within a particular life-context. Questions of the former kind belong to the realm of *Moralität*, the sphere of discourse ethics, while the latter belong to the realm of *Sittlichkeit*.[23]

IV Habermas and Rawls

Discourse ethics is an "ethics of suspicion,"[24] incorporating the skepticism implicit in the definition of modernity which must, in accord with the basic canons of the position, generate itself out of itself without recourse to tradition. Although the foray into ethics may be seen for some as a point of departure from the theory of communicative action, the basic parameters of ethical theory have been established through that very theory. This leads to interesting consequences. For example, whereas Habermas and Rawls were allies in the seventies, the Rawls who has accommodated to the critiques of the communitarians in the eighties is quite different from the Habermas who is bound by the restrictions set down in the theory of communicative action. Modernity has been defined as that which must generate the structures of normativity out of itself. The wager is that that can be done with a theory of rationality based on language. Given the general desire to transform issues of the philosophy of consciousness into the philosophy of language, it will be necessary to develop ethics out of language. The argument must follow characteristic patterns; according to the canons of modernity, an ethical position must be generated without recourse to tradition in the sense that it must absent itself from recourse to particular traditions to justify itself. The assumption is that the logic of discursive procedures can do just that. For instance, the presupposition is that certain procedures which inform the logic of discourse will enable the development of a consensus regarding the proper adjudication of validity claims. These procedures must be read out of the nature of discourse and

---

[22] Habermas maintains that his discourse ethics is open to a "pluralism" of values requiring agreement on normative principles only.

[23] See W. Kuhlmann, ed. *Moralität und Sittlichkeit* (Frankfurt am Main, Suhrkamp, 1986).

[24] I choose the phrase "ethics of suspicion" with care. In principle, a discourse ethics is suspicious of all possible reliance on tradition for the determination of moral categories. Even traditions, such as modern democratic ones, which have provided a climate for the acceptance of the proceduralism endorsed by the discourse ethic have to be looked at with suspicion.

not from particular forms of cultural agreement. If the latter were the case, the very claims of modernity would be aborted. It is in this sense that discursive ethics, that is, an ethics based on a theory of language, conforms to a particular view of the nature of modernity.

Some would want to see this as the great virtue of discourse ethics, namely, to have located an ethical position based upon procedures of discourse − freeing ethical discourse from traditional considerations. Others would, of course, see this as an absurd attempt to leap, as it were, out of one's historical skin. What both critics and supporters of Habermas have failed to see is that the logic of the position limits modification, particularly in the light of communitarian or quasi-communitarian critique. In other words, Habermas does not enjoy Rawls's luxury of succumbing to at least part of the criticism of the communitarians by accepting the claim that modern notions of justice are informed by modern liberal traditions.[25] On the contrary, Habermas is pretty much forced to read out of the structures of discourse procedures which will grant, on the basis of language itself, the categories of emancipation.[26] In other words, the very canons of the position Habermas has developed, which incorporates the suspicion of cultural forms implicit in his definition of modernity, restrict the definition of discourse ethics on this level. This may be either a virtue or a vice, depending upon one's point of view. What is significant is that Habermas, rather than acquiescing to the critiques of the communitarians, attempts instead to strengthen the universalist position through the exercise of reconstructive science.

V The Strong Claims of the Discourse Ethic

Discourse ethics may be said to provide a procedural justification for truth and validity claims. When one speaks of something being valid, one assumes

[25] Rawls has at least partially responded to the critiques of Sandel and others, who suggest that the very arguments he has defended are dependent upon liberal traditions. Hence, his argument can be reconstructed as an historical argument. However, Rawls's position need not be reduced to a communitarian one. For an excellent interpretative defense of Rawls on this point, see Richard Rorty. "The Priority of Democracy to Philosophy" in *The Virginia Statute of Religious Freedom*, eds Merrill Paterson and Robert Vaughan (Cambridge, Cambridge University Press, 1987), pp. 257−82.

[26] The word "forced" may reflect a rather extreme descriptive choice on my part. The point is that by developing this rather strong anti-contextualist position as reflected both in the reading of modernity (the rational position must generate itself out of itself), and the construction of the theory of communicative action on the so-called scientific claims of language itself, Habermas would have to abandon much of his position if he acquiesced to the arguments of the communitarians.

a certain background consensus presupposing comprehensibility, truth, correctness or appropriateness, truthfulness or authenticity.[27] The aim of discourse is to generate a rationally motivated consensus. Over the years, Habermas has argued that such a consensus presupposes an ideal speech situation as a kind of meta-norm, a situation which, in turn, assumes a certain kind of symmetry and reciprocity. The symmetry is associated with an equal chance both to initiate communication and to make assertions, while the reciprocity refers to an equal opportunity to make wishes and feelings known, and to provide an assurance that the chances will be equally distributed. Inasmuch as the aim of discourse is to generate rationally motivated consensus − and one can construct the conditions whereby that consensus occurs − one has demonstrated, in the process, the fundamental character of discursive rationality. The consensus theory of truth and validity is essentially cognitive. What Habermas has attempted to show is that normative statements admit of cognitive validation. The assumption of a discourse ethics is that one can show how cognitive validation occurs essentially by reconstructing the procedure for justifying norms. It is here that the ideal speech situation comes into play as a normative justification procedure presupposing rationality, justice (in terms of the equality spoken of above), and freedom, in the sense that the only force is the force of the better argument.[28]

As critics have pointed out, discourse itself cannot be the mere embodiment of the claims of a cognitivist ethic; the locus of moral judgment must also be represented in individuals who are competent or capable of engaging in consensus at the very refined level that Habermas suggests. Hence, Habermas argues that the reconstructions of discourse ethics are complemented by developmental psychology according to Kohlberg. The claim is that communicative ethics offers a "privileged description" of post-conventional[29] moral reasoning. Habermas asserts that these kinds of descriptive procedures are associated with a post-conventional morality which has been institutionalized in the modern world. Hence, here, as in the case of

---

[27] These four categories originate in the essay "What Is Universal Pragmatics?".

[28] For a good discussion of Habermas's position on ethics in relationship to political theory, see Steven K. White *The Recent Work of Jürgen Habermas*. (Cambridge, Cambridge University Press, 1987).

[29] Habermas, following Kohlberg, argues for three stages, in the broad sense, of moral reasoning; the pre-conventional, the conventional, and the post-conventional. Significantly, the post-conventional level of moral reasoning, with its focus on the moral autonomy of the individual, is said to be correlative with the aims of a discourse ethic. Kohlberg's enterprise in cognitive psychology as a reconstructive science would serve to provide a practical affirmation of discourse ethics. In this sense, discourse ethics provides a "privileged access" to a post-conventional morality.

the theory of communicative action generally, the old arguments of epistemology are replaced by the new insights of reconstructive science. The conditions for the possibility of ethical activity (judgment) are given on the basis of a certain moral know-how present in the modern ethical subject.[30]

VI The Hegelian Critique

As I suggested at the outset of this discussion, the communitarian critique of the universalist position began essentially with Hegel. One could argue that the major critiques of this position, whether in Walzer, MacIntyre, Sandel, Williams, Nussbaum or others, have more or less been anticipated in Hegel's critique of the Kantian position. There is essentially one major point in that critique which, already implicit in Aristotle, Hegel developed from his early analysis of Greek culture, namely, that the principles of rationality are already embedded within the development of culture. In the *Nichomachean Ethics*, Aristotle required no meta-ethical principles, no practice of universalization, no principle of equality in order that virtue be achieved. Virtue was essentially a practice which was to be won through the art of imitation by those who were not only willing to pursue excellence, but also could find one whose excellence was known and who could, therefore, be appropriately imitated. Of course, Hegel understood that the basic assumptions about Greek culture could no longer hold; however, he would maintain the identification as embedded within a specific cultural form.[31]

As Seyla Benhabib suggests, discourse ethics in its reliance on the Kantian-like principle of universalizability is subject to a critique modeled on Hegel's critique of Kant. As she asserts, echoing MacIntyre's critique of Kant, the incorporation of the universalizability principle is at best inconsistent and at worst tautological. Discourse ethics suggests that only those norms which meet with the consensus of all in practical discourse can claim validity. Benhabib finds that the need for the universalizability principle, which, she argues, is not essential to communicative ethics, is perceived as necessary to avoid "consensual violation," a problem as old as

[30] If the Kohlbergian analysis is correct, it follows that what were heretofore epistemological arguments can be articulated on practical grounds independent of epistemological reference. The argument cited above is parallel to the one which calls for a division of spheres into the scientific, moral and aesthetic on Weber's notion of differentiated cultural value spheres. In the later Habermas, epistemology re-emerges as practice.

[31] Hegel would argue, on the basis of his philosophy of history, that the process of universalization is implicit within culture.

modern political philosophy itself. She states: "In order to avoid the un-
desirable consequence that participants in a discourse may adopt principles
which would contradict the very principles of discourse itself, it becomes
necessary to define the rules of discursive argumentation."[32] No doubt, this
is a key problem. Anticipating Hegel's critique of Kant, Benhabib argues
that universalizability is only possible on the basis of certain other assumptions. In other words, rather than universalizability being simply derived
from the principle of practical reason, as Kant would have it, this principle
is itself based on the institutionalization of reason. Jack Mendelson, as
Benhabib observes, states the dilemma rather well:

The historical potential of the ideal speech situation for becoming the actual
organizing principle of society can only come to fruition in a society which comes
close to articulating it on the level of more historically specific and conscious
traditions, for instance, the Western democracies of the twentieth century. While in
a sense the ideal of rational consensus may be immanent in language *per se* and not
simply an external standard, in most societies it is bound to remain unarticulated in
the actual culture. It becomes politically relevant as an ideal to be consciously
striven for only in societies which have begun to approach it on the level of their
own cultural traditions.[33]

Mendelson's point is well taken. Here we see remnants of a Habermas,
encountered earlier, who, in the name of science and rational argumentation,
incorporates principles which are implicit in a certain social and political
orientation toward the world. For Benhabib, however, the issue is a more
subtle one. It is really a question of whether or not Habermas's way of
presenting the principle of universalization, implicit in a communicative
ethics without recourse to actual practice, is appropriate.

Communicative ethics demands from its participants a *willingness* and *ability* to
consider normative questions from a universalist standpoint and to regard every
being as an equal regardless of the actual constellation of relations in real life. Even
if we admit that such willingness and such ability emerge out of contingent circumstances, there is a dilemma here. The necessity of discursive argumentation arises
when, through conflict and crisis, social and political agents challenge an established
background consensus.[34]

The point is a challenging one. The real dilemmas regarding consensus

---

[32] Seyla Benhabib, *Critique, Norm and Utopia* (New York, Columbia University Press,
1986), p. 303.
[33] Jack Mendelson, "The Habermas–Gadamer Debate", *New German Critique*; quoted in
Benhabib.
[34] Ibid., 320–1.

arise, given this view, not at the abstract level of universalization, but at the concrete level of conflict and resolution. Benhabib continues: "Yet the very step of 'abstraction' that leads such agents to engage in discourse, namely, the *virtualization* of the constraints of action, can only take place when such agents are willing to *suspend* the motivating force and content of these real conflict situations." Reflecting a kind of Schutzian insight into the nature of the lifeworld, Benhabib makes the very interesting point that "Discourses arise when the intersubjectivity of ethical life is *endangered*; but the very project of discursive argumentation presupposes the ongoing validity of a *reconciled* intersubjectivity."[35]

To be sure, Habermas seeks another line for the development of communicative ethics reflected in his distinction between morality and ethical life, namely, to distinguish between principles of moral justification and those of contextualization.[36] The Hegelian overtones of Benhabib's critique are obvious. In principle, reason cannot be separated from life practice without violating the very form and content of rational appropriation. From here it is only a short step to make the critique of Habermas not only from the point of view of Hegel, but also from the perspective of earlier critical theory, namely, that a communicative ethics is impossible if dissociated from life struggle. As Benhabib observes, the problem is one of the proper definition of reason. Whereas Kant could not show how reason could be a "motive for action," for Hegel reason shapes and gives content to desire. If one works out the practical implications of Hegel's critique, questions of justice cannot be separated from those of happiness. In the end, Benhabib pleads for a kind of transformation of communicative ethics into one open to life struggle, on the one hand, and its utopian content, on the other, in a manner not unlike the approach of an earlier version of critical theory.

VII Habermas's Response to the Communitarians

It is one short step from this kind of criticism, which emphasizes context over modes of justification, to the neo-Aristotelianism which characterizes the contemporary ethical critiques of universalism carried on by such philosophers as MacIntyre, Taylor, Williams, and Wiggins. In a recent paper, Habermas addresses what he considers to be three major objections to his position or, more generally, "moral theories of a Kantian type," which can be made from a neo-Aristotelian perspective. Of course, Aristotle

[35] Ibid., p. 321.

[36] For an excellent analysis of this distinction, as well as an additional development, see Klaus Günther, *Der Sinn für Angemessenheit: Anwendungsdiskurse in Moral und Recht*, (Frankfurt am Main, Suhrkamp, 1988).

raised the question of moral action from the perspective of the question of the good while separating "practical reason from theory proper."[37]

Habermas believes that, with the rise of modern science, the whole question of the relationship of morality to science must be readdressed because of the decline of Aristotelian metaphysics, on the one hand, and the rise of the critique – perhaps one should say the undermining – of morality, on the other. Kant, operating without Aristotelian metaphysical assumptions, addresses the question of the possibility of moral reasoning in modern society. He inaugurates the "moral point of view" from which we can "impartially ... decide between narrative claims on the basis of good reasons." From Habermas's perspective, the neo-Aristotelian critiques suggest that Kant paid too high a "price" for "the concept of an autonomous, post-metaphysical morality."[38] They make three criticisms of the so-called Kantian "abstraction." The first has to do with motivation. Kant, in developing the moral point of view, distinguished between the good and that which was the right and proper thing to do. Only the latter was considered to be in the proper domain of morality; the former, the question of the good, was reduced to the realm of empirical preference. In so doing, the point of classical ethics, namely, how one should live one's life, was lost. Briefly, neo-Aristotelian critique suggests that Kant undercut the ground for moral motivation. Why be moral in the first place?

Second, the neo-Aristotelian critique suggests that Kant made a false abstraction from the practical situation. Kant, by making a distinction between contextualization and justification, left open the question of making a choice between competing norms. "Such a model cuts moral reasoning down to justification and does not do justice to the fact that the application of principles and the choice between competing norms do pose problems of their own."[39]

Third, the Kantian moral point of view abstracts from, or eliminates, reflection on communal life. Again, as neo-Aristotelians are wont to show, this leads to problems. "The first is an atomistic concept of person leaving the free will" separated "from every social bond that gives life its meaning."[40] Beyond that, given the plurality of communities in the modern world, it is difficult to see how any claim for universality can be made.

In summary, the claims of the neo-Aristotelian perspective amounts to the following:

---

[37] Jürgen Habermas, "Kohlberg and Neo-Aristotelianism", 1988, p. 6. All citations are from the manuscript to be published in the journal *New Directions for Child Development*.
[38] Ibid., p. 7.
[39] Ibid., p. 11.
[40] Ibid.

The deontological focus on what one ought to do demands a strict separation between the right and the good, between obligation and desire. This leads to an *abstraction from motivation* and leaves the question "Why be moral?" unanswered. The *cognitivist* focus on the level of post-conventional reasoning brings the question of justification to the fore. This leads to an *abstraction of the particular situation* and ignores the independent logic of questions of application. The *formalistic* focus on universality goes together with an atomistic concept of the person and a contractarian view of society. This leads to an *abstraction from the ethical life of particular communities* and raises doubt about the possibility of a strict distinction between form and content and a context-independent conceptualization of justice.[41]

Now, to the defense of the moral perspective. Regarding the first point, that about motivation, Habermas believes that one can resolve the problem only by rehabilitating the metaphysical claims of Aristotle's ethics in a world where there is a plurality of values. In this view, MacIntyre represents the dilemma of trying to dismiss Aristotle's "metaphysical biology," which ascertains one specific form of life, and at the same time mustering "many varieties of practices and traditions and of narrative accounts of a single human life without ever reaching one single set of distinguishing features of the good."[42]

Regarding the second question, the question of context, Habermas argues that "if we take modern pluralism seriously we have to abstain from the claim that philosophy can spell out an excellent mode of life."[43] It is Habermas's claim that if one considers a position like Williams's, which perceives the limits of philosophic reasoning in modernity, while still attempting to use *phronesis* as a kind of guide to life's ethical choices, one discovers another set of problems. In Williams's sense, ethical reflection can modify practice. But, claims Habermas, if ethical reflection modifies practice one is led to the question of universalization, i.e., right back to the Kantian posing of the question. "*Phronesis* without metaphysical backing must, under modern conditions, either dissolve into flat common sense, or develop into a practical reason that meets the criteria of procedural rationality."[44]

The third question, that of abstraction from a particular form of life (in Aristotle the question of the *polis*), leads to the most obvious critique of all. Given the plurality of modern life forms, reflection on a particular form of life leads to a critical acceptance of that form. "Finally, if we remain

[41] Ibid., pp. 12–13.
[42] Ibid., p. 14. Independent of whether this critique of the Neo-Aristotelian position is valid, it is difficult to see how the problem of motivation is thereby solved from the Kantian-cognitivist point of view.
[43] Ibid.
[44] Ibid.

faithful to the Aristotelian view that moral reasoning is bounded by the law of the city, and [if we] remain linked to a lived-in ethos, we must be prepared to dispense with the emancipatory potential of moral universalism and abandon the chance for a penetrating moral criticism of exploitative and repressive social structures."[45] Habermas points to Charles Taylor's attempt to answer this criticism. Taylor's examples are taken from Plato, the Stoics, and Christianity. While Habermas acknowledges their presence as "pacemakers for moral universalism," he argues that "their ontological and religious premises might be even less compatible with post-metaphysical thought than those of Aristotle." Beyond that, in the German context, the conservation of certain life forms has always represented a certain form of conservatism and, in the contemporary context, neo-conservatism.

After pointing to the limitations of the motivational, contextual, and life-form critiques as presented by neo-Aristotelianism, rather than dismiss them, Habermas argues that they can be incorporated into a post-Kantian form of deontological ethics. With regard to the question of motivation, the deontological point, Habermas argues, *vis-à-vis* examples from Lawrence Kohlberg, that people are quite capable of distinguishing questions of context from questions of moral justification. Beyond that, he argues that there is no reason to assume that a moral theory should motivate people to act. As usual, Habermas is quite happy to resign himself to a minimalist ethical position, "To know the right answer to a moral problem means that nobody has a good reason to act otherwise." And then he adds, somewhat ironically, "This may not be much, but it is more than nothing. Moral judgments do possess just the degree of motivating force which the reasons possess on which they rest; and that degree varies with persons and contexts."[46]

With regard to the question of abstraction from a particular situation, the cognitivist point, Habermas defends a strong interpretation of the distinction between justification and application. Kant is interpreted here as not having been radical enough. "To know which norms and principles are valid is not yet sufficient for knowing how I shall act in a particular situation."[47] One presumes he would stand by the point made earlier, that in modernity *phronesis* leads to questions of universalization.

Finally, turning to the question of abstraction from a form of life, the formalist point, Habermas agrees that the radical atomization of the individual, as envisaged by Kant, must be countered by a concept of intersubjectivity, as present in Hegel and the American pragmatist tradition.

---

[45] Ibid., p. 16.

[46] Ibid., p. 20. Clearly this statement doesn't really solve the problem of motivation. However, Habermas is quite willing to let it stand as such.

[47] Ibid.

Consequently, it is not necessary to re-introduce the concept of teleology in order to rehabilitate the notion of the individual from a neo-Aristotelian point of view. Rather, argues Habermas, and one might expect this, "The reconstruction has . . . to start from the model of communicative action."[48]

Has Habermas really slain the communitarian dragon while incorporating its criticism? If there is one criticism that cuts across all three character-izations made of the communitarian critique of Habermas, it would be that the deontological, the cognitivist, and the formalistic positions taken by the discourse ethic presume that one can entertain the illusion of departing from the world of everyday life in order to construct a world in which one can ideally abstract from conditions of motivation, of particularity, and of life form. The critics would seem almost united regarding one point, namely, the very structure of the tripartite abstraction which Habermas makes is informed by the character of a particular life form. Whether one makes this claim in terms of the distinction between virtual and actual, the distinction between practical life and utopia, or the distinction between *phronesis* and modern rationality, there is a kind of critical unity which suggests that Habermas never answers fully the critiques of the communitarians.

With regard to the first abstraction, the abstraction of motivation, Haber-mas claims, as we have seen, "to know the right answer to a moral problem means that nobody has a good reason to act otherwise." Some would want to suggest that *knowledge* of the right answer cannot be merely derived from the rules of argumentation. Indeed, this is precisely where the debate would begin. If knowledge were not gained from some type of concrete, contextual experience of life, would it not be trivial knowledge? One would presume that Habermas wants to deny this. But would not denial of a trivial answer on this level entail the use of some concept of *phronesis*, some kind of understanding of life gained from practical experience? In fact, of course, behind this critique lurks the suspicion that indeed, in terms of the motivational abstraction, the claims of the discourse ethic are not, after all, that abstract. That is to say, they owe their origin to a particular form of life experience characteristic of modern Western democ-racy in its various manifestations.

In a peculiar way, Habermas acknowledges this, not on the level of a kind of modern *phronesis*, but rather on the level of reconstructive science, the substitute for *phronesis* in the Habermasian world-view. If, for example, one is able to know the right answer to a moral problem, it is because of the development of a certain moral character at the level of a post-conventional morality.

[48] Ibid., p. 24.

If the first point, abstraction from motivation, is questionable, the second, the contextual, is also questionable. Is it really possible to separate questions of justification from questions of application, or is it not the case that the very orientation toward universalization is derived from a culture of pluralism? Habermas's critique of Bernard Williams is telling in this regard. Habermas refers to Williams's attempt to find a form of ethical reflection which "would help us to find our way around in a social world which ... was shown to be the best social world for human beings."[49] Habermas argues that, if this is the case, one would find a kind of ethical reflection which coincides directly "with an intersubjectivist interpretation of Kant's practical reason."[50] In other words, one would be led to a position which, in the name of procedures of universalization, would separate questions of justification from those of application. But if procedures of universalization are already given within the modern culture of pluralism, it is difficult to see how there can be a pure separation between the two modes, inasmuch as the context for universalization is already given within the culture. Habermas argues that "knowledge of which norms and principles are valid is not yet sufficient for knowing how I shall act in a particular situation. The process of application escapes the procedure of universalization."[51] But is this really the case? Could it not be precisely the opposite, namely, that the very question of wanting to know which norms are valid does not arise until one is acting within a particular situation? It is not that questions of universalization are not posed; rather they are posed within the context of practical life itself.

The third point, the one about formalism and ethical life would, as it were, be subject to the same critique. As Wellmer[52] and others have argued, the very formalization which Habermas attempts to sustain is one that is not far from the context of ethical life. Habermas takes the chief charge against formalism to be its atomistic concept of the person. His assumption is that if one reconstructs the subject (the Kantian autonomous individual) vis-à-vis the insights of pragmatism, one can retain the Kantian notion of the individual while at the same time preserving the universalism in Kantian formalism. Here, the argument begins to have a neo-Aristotelian ring to it. "Peirce and Mead developed the idea of a universal community or a universal discourse that can serve as an instance of appeal beyond existing communities without losing the essential features of a communal praxis. In the notion of the *ideal* role-taking this notion of a *transcending*

---

[49] Bernard Williams, *Ethics and the Limits of Philosophy* (London, 1985); quoted in Habermas, Ibid., p. 15.

[50] Ibid.

[51] Ibid., p. 20.

[52] Albrecht Wellmer, *Ethik und Dialog* (Frankfurt am Main, Suhrkamp, 1986).

community is preserved."[53] One would want to know, of course, just how transcendent such a community is. If it is possible to suggest that forms of universality are present in modern life, then is not this form of idealization already present in modern experience? Habermas argues that the ideal communication community contains elements which are essentially independent from more "repressive" forms of life present in modern communal experience. Hence, the ideal communication community can abstract from the more contingent characteristics of modern experience. But is not such an abstraction already implicit in the very structure of modern experience?

There are two issues here: the first concerns the validity of the ideal speech situation associated with the notion of communicative action, while the second concerns the necessity of such a theory. Is the Kantian method of argumentation not itself dependent on the implicit universalization characteristic of modern cultures? Is it not the case that Kant really builds into his theory of rationality basic political assumptions which are already present in the development of modern democracies? And, if that is the case, is the apparatus assumed by grounding the conditions of argumentation in the idealized assumptions regarding communication really necessary? Marx was forever satirizing German thought by pointing out that Germans had to achieve in theory what other countries had achieved in actuality. History may have a way of repeating itself.

VIII Discourse Ethics and the Dilemmas of Language

In the end, of course, Habermas anticipates potential onslaughts by the communitarians, who provide the major challenge to his position, on grounds which are fairly consistently established on the basis of his theory of communicative action on the one hand, and his theory of modernity on the other. However, would he really have us believe that the communitarian thesis, with its emancipatory overtones, is implicit in the nature of discourse as such, independent of specific forms of life? The tension between the theory of modernity and the philosophy of language manifests itself here as well. Let me suggest that Habermas may not be able to have his deontological cake, with its cognitive-formalist icing, and eat it too. Again, we are back to problems indigenous to the theory of communicative action itself. The problem is simply this: can one sustain the claim that basic assumptions regarding the communicative resolution of truth and validity are given in language as discourse?

[53] Jürgen Habermas, "Kohlberg and Neo-Aristotelianism," p. 23.

Ernst Tugendhat[54] has raised this problem by posing the question: is the fundamental thesis with regard to communication really given in language? Habermas's fundamental claim in the discourse ethics is that the logic of argumentation shows that the rules of argumentation are communicative. Tugendhat is quite aware from whence the communicative thesis comes, namely, from Peirce's attempt to deal with the nature of truth in empirical science. For Tugendhat one could say that progress in empirical science is communicative but that progress in empirical science is not designated by rules. That is to say that, where communication is concerned, the question is not cognition but voluntary association. In terms of language, one can say that the so-called rules of ideal speech cannot be internalized, i.e., not considered as the internal semantic structure of language. From Tugendhat's point of view the only way to think of the idea of a communicative ethic is in combination with the idea of democracy. In this sense, communicative ethics has nothing directly to do with language.

This raises the question of just how far Habermas has avoided the communitarian critique. To be sure, if the basic theses of communitarian ethics are really derived from radical democracy, then has not Habermas indulged in the very procedure that he declared taboo for others, namely, has he not selected a particular tradition from which to argue and sustain his ethical point of view?

[54] Ernst Tugendhat, *Probleme der Ethik* (Stuttgart, Philip Reclam, 1984). This criticism refers to the original criticism of the theory of communicative action by Tugendhat and Zimmermann.

5

Communication and the Law

I Between Justification and Application

What is the relationship between morality and law? Law contextualizes morality in the sense that ideally the non-contextual procedures of morality find their application in law. In the overall Habermasian scheme of things, morality is related to the question of justification, while law and politics are related to the question of application.[1] Briefly, law is to morality as application is to justification.

Allow me return to the point taken up in the previous chapter regarding the distinction Habermas makes between morality and ethical life. Habermas begins by reconstructing Kant's version of the categorical imperative considering the general linguistic constructs implied in the theory of communicative action. Setting aside my general reservations about the overall success of this attempt, one could justify the basic universalist assumptions which are implied in moral theory through the general framework of a discourse ethic. The theory attempts to distinguish morality from ethical life by arguing that questions of morality are deontological, formal, and cognitive, while questions of ethical life are essentially questions of contextuality. Behind this distinction between ethics and morality which foreshadows that between law and morality, lies, as if presupposed by the cunning of reason, a scheme accounting for the relationship between morality, law, ethics, and politics. As soon as one attempts to distinguish between law and morality such a scheme is implied, particularly when one writes, as Habermas does, in the shadow of Kant, Hegel, and Weber.

The question of the relationship between law and morality not only presumes the German enlightenment and post-enlightenment way of posing the question, but also the vigorous contemporary discussion of the place of the law in the context of liberal, conservative, and critical perspectives. The question of the relationship between law and morality can be answered in

Parts of this chapter were originally published in *Praxis International*. David M. Rasmussen. "Communication Theory and the Critique of the Law," vol. 8, 1988, no. 2. pp. 155–70. Reprinted by permission of the publisher.

[1] For an excellent discussion of the problem of application, see Klaus Günther, *Der Sinn für Angemessenheit: Anwendungsdiskurse in Moral und Recht* (Frankfurt am Main, Suhrkamp, 1988).

many ways. One could state that this question is really one of the status of the moral law (Kant),[2] that morality is really implicit in the law (Hegel),[3] that law is essentially independent of morality (Weber and legal positivism),[4] that the law really raises problems of morality as a matter of principle (Dworkin),[5] that legal questions are fundamentally indeterminate and therefore either matters of social policy,[6] reconstructive social theory,[7] or deconstructive social analysis[8] (the three versions of critical legal theory). It appears that Habermas, on the basis of insights derived from the construction of the theory of communicative action, on the one hand, and discourse ethics on the other, attempts to construct a distinctive answer to the question combined with, to be sure, a heavy reliance on the German enlightenment. Habermas is Kantian in his attempt to clarify that which has a universalistic claim in relationship to the law, while, at the same time, he is Hegelian, reflecting the strategy of Hegel's *Rechtsphilosophie* in his attempt to show the relationship between morality, law, ethics, politics, and ultimately the role of the state in modern society. And, as we shall see, near the end of this discussion, his discourse fits rather nicely into the context of current debates regarding the status of the law in modern society.

II Law and Morality

If one were to read Max Weber's discourses on law quite carefully, it would be possible to come to a conclusion that is the opposite of Hegel's, namely, that as law began to be separated from its origins in religious traditions it emancipated itself from morality. As such, Weber's work on

[2] The problem with Kant's moral theory is that it incorporates law in such a manner that the distinction between law and morality is obliterated.

[3] Hegel is much more empirical than Kant. He attempts, in his *Rechtsphilosophie*, to work from actual statutes to general propositions about the law.

[4] Weber is more or less willing to let the assumptions of legal positivism stand. Legal positivism assumed that the traditional and presumed line between law and morality could be severed.

[5] Dworkin, in his earlier work, attempted to find the principle of morality as a principle within the law itself. His recent work has taken a more hermeneutic turn. Hence, as I will show at the end of this chapter, he raises serious questions about both the need for and the status of moral universalism as applied to law.

[6] This position of legal indeterminacy is one associated with the first generation of the Critical Legal Studies movement led by Duncan Kennedy. I will deal with this position in relation to that of Habermas later in this chapter.

[7] I refer here to the so-called prophetic side of Critical Legal Studies associated with Roberto Unger.

[8] Deconstructionist legal studies are associated with the most recent development of Critical Legal Studies under David Kennedy and others.

the law constitutes the negative case for a discourse which attempts to unite law and morality. Weber's rather massive work on the law gave rise to a single question, namely, how is legal domination in modern society possible? Since modern societies owe their origin to the rule of law, what is it that legitimates such rule? Weber's "sociological" explanation sought to show that as law differentiated itself from its religious foundations it sought to free itself from questions of morality, seeking rather its legitimacy in reference to itself on the basis of properties within the law. Law became the exclusive realm of professionals. This professionalization of law had its correlation in its formalization, i.e., a system of procedures which are known to professionals only. In turn, legitimization was referable to the particular form of rationality employed by professional jurists, a "value-free" rationality distinct from morality.[9]

To be sure, for this kind of analysis, Weber is something of an easy target inasmuch as the critique of Weber's sociology of law becomes part and parcel of the critique of "value-free" rationality which can be quite easily shown to mask, rather than rise above, the interests of those who employ it. As Justice Holmes has pointed out, every opinion tends to become a law.[10] Indeed, as we know now, law functions in the interests of those who make it, as the Warren and Burger courts have shown.[11] Yet, this unmasking does not lead to the proposition that law is a "sham"[12] because of its association with particular interests; rather, it leads to a judgment about the association of law with morality. Habermas concludes with an alternative claim: "The formal properties of law studied by Weber could have granted the legitimacy of legality only under specific social conditions and only insofar as they were 'rational' in a moral-practical sense."[13] The Habermasian critique, then, with its assumptions about the distinction between justification and application, assumes that the Weberian analysis really depends upon a certain confusion, i.e., "He falsely identifies

---

[9] Habermas, interpreting Weber, states: "Legal domination acquires a rational character in that, among other things, belief in the legality of authorities and enacted regulations has a quality different from that of belief in tradition or charisma. *It is the rationality intrinsic to the form of law itself that secures the legitimacy of power exercised in legal forms.*" Jürgen Habermas, "Law and Morality: Two Lectures", *The Tanner Lectures VIII*, ed. Sterling M. McMurrin, (Salt Lake City, University of Utah Press, 1987), p. 219. (Emphasis mine.)

[10] Holmes was one of the first to challenge legal positivism by pointing out that what appeared to be a sanctioning of positive principles was simply an appeal to popular economic theory. His dissenting opinion in *Lochner* vs. *New York* makes the case in point.

[11] Different courts can be said to reflect different orientations and opinions as such. The Rehnquist court makes this point rather dramatically.

[12] The question of whether or not law is a sham reflects the identification of law and social policy characteristic of the original Critical Legal Studies movement.

[13] Jürgen Habermas, *The Tanner Lectures*, p. 227.

the procedural properties of a post-traditional level of justification with substantive values."[14] Habermas, having earlier made, as we have seen, the distinction between morality and ethics, cashes in on that distinction by claiming that procedures can be distinguished from substantial value orientations. Procedures are associated with a post-conventional level of justification, while substantive value orientations can be associated with the "content" of the law. If one grants the distinction, one can claim that there is a certain relationship established between morality and the law. Procedures are associated with levels of universalization which constitute the deontological, formal, and cognitive characteristics of morality. Inasmuch as law cannot be legitimized independently of certain procedures, law, in a post-conventional society, cannot exist independently of that element of morality as represented in the procedures that bring it about. This view in turn foreshadows a certain understanding of the relationship of law, ethics, politics, and the state, where the procedural justification implicit in both the legislative and judicial processes will provide the necessary link between actual political processes and morality in the name of procedural rationality.

Habermas goes on to claim that, precisely because Weber equates procedure with substantive value orientations, "He does not see that the model of the social contract (in a way similar to the categorical imperative) can be understood as proposing a procedure whose rationality is supposed to guarantee the correctness of whatever decisions come about in a procedural manner."[15] The point of this somewhat surprising statement is that there is, according to Habermas's most recent argumentation, a certain truth in modern natural law theory which can more or less be redeemed by modern communicative "procedural" rationality.

If one were to take the case of Hobbes, for example, it is conceivable that the argument in the thirteenth chapter of *The Leviathan*, with its appeal to modalities of universality articulated in the law of nature, which are in turn guaranteed in the social contract, presents one with an early understanding of the relationship of a universal rationality, as implicit in the use of certain procedures, to the substantial character of the law, as generated within this early view of contractarian society. In other words, it could be argued that that which legitimates law *vis-à-vis* the social contract is the guarantee of the rationality of the procedural process for its attainment,

---

[14] Ibid., p. 228. Here, both Weber's analysis and its critique focus on a specific form of legal theory, namely legal positivism. The critique reflects an extension of the notion of "formal pragmatics," which Habermas works out elsewhere. In principle, the concept of procedure presumes an implicit appeal to a certain form of rationality. Here, this notion is extended to account for legal procedure.

[15] Ibid.

which incorporates certain universal assumptions. To put it quite simply, for Hobbes, the guarantee for entering into society is the granting of a certain universal equality.[16]

In any case, according to this argument, what Max Weber seems to have missed, in his history of the reading of law, was the meaning of the concept of legal procedure. Ultimately, the question of legal procedure cannot be isolated from a specific form of law when one considers the relationship of law to moral-practical rationality in general. For Habermas, the generality derived from this analysis is the following: "Legitimacy is possible on the basis of legality insofar as the procedures for the production and application of legal norms are also conducted reasonably, in the moral-practical sense of procedural rationality."[17]

As we shall see, that implies a certain view, not only of law and morality and their relationship, but also of the democratic order. In other words, law can only legitimate itself in a society where procedural rationality has, more or less, been institutionalized. But again, as with morality itself, Habermas argues that this is not a contextualist argument. Rather, following Kant instead of Hegel at this point, Habermas asserts that legitimation of the law occurs on the basis of certain procedures guaranteed by post-conventional rationality.

However, if the connection of law and morality has been suggested, the precise place of procedure in relation to the development of law has yet to be articulated. Surprisingly, it is an historical mode of analysis, proposed as a thought experiment, which provides the basis for the theoretical assumption about procedural rationality and the law. Habermas makes the case that in traditional societies the link between sacred and secular is provided by the "moment of indisponibility," the necessary legitimation, for the law. The term "indisponibility" refers to the fact that sacred law was not simply determined by the whim of the political ruler. "This divine, or natural, law was *not at the disposal* of the political ruler; in this sense it was *indisponible (unverfügbar)*."[18] From this, one can draw the following conclusion: "The canopy of sacred law provided the legitimating context within which the ruler exercised his [or her] secular power through the functions of adjudication and bureaucratic legislation."[19] Accordingly, it is this moment, the moment of indisponibility, which provides the link between law and morality. The thought experiment proposed suggests that, under the most

[16] Rolf Zimmermann has made this point quite effectively in "Equality, Political Order and Ethics," in *Philosophy and Social Criticism*, 14:3/4 (Summer, 1989.)

[17] Habermas, *The Tanner Lectures*, p. 230.

[18] Ibid., p. 261.

[19] Ibid.

archaic conditions, the tribal chief could rely on "the morally binding force of intersubjectively recognized legal norms."[20] It is this reliance on intersubjectively binding norms which is transferred to the judge and eventually to the legitimate ruler, where the "instrumental aspect of law" exists "alongside the aspect of the indisponibility of traditional law."[21] Hence, the conclusion: "For this scenario, morality functions as a catalyst in the fusion of compulsory law and political power."[22]

In other words, as law developed, the idea of natural law tended to take the place of the sacred as that which preserved the moment of indisponibility, legitimizing secular law. As natural law theories broke down, that moment was preserved in reference to procedural rationality, a reference which preserved the moment of indisponibility, present in the original association between sacred and secular law, by finding the modalities for legitimation outside the law itself. Consequently, if this is the case, one has defeated the assumptions in Weber's separation of positive law in particular and legal positivism generally, namely, that law functions independently from morality.

III   Law and Communicative Action

One can now link the theory of the relationship of law and morality in Habermas's thought with the theory of communicative action. If the link between law and morality is to be found in adherence to procedures, it does not follow that procedures have always been properly endorsed. In essence, the thesis about the relationship between law and morality is as critical as it is constructive. I take it to be no accident that *The Tanner Lectures* conclude by stating: "There can be no autonomous law without the realization of democracy."[23] The statement can be read in two ways: either, because clear evidence exists of democratic procedure in autonomous law, there can be no autonomous law without a realized democracy, or, because autonomous law *lacks* evidence of democratic procedures, there can be no autonomous law without a realized democracy.[24] What Habermas has done is to provide us with a way of looking at the law from developmental and contemporary perspectives which will be both effectively critical and, at the same time, ground the legitimacy of this view.

[20] Ibid., p. 266.
[21] Ibid.
[22] Ibid.
[23] Ibid., p. 279.
[24] No matter which way one reads this statement the link between law and morality is established theoretically.

One can put the above discussion in the context of communicative action by appealing to the debate regarding *juridification*, i.e., the proliferation of processes of legalization that have occurred in the modern, post-1600, period of social history.[25] In systematic terms, the theory of communicative action conceives of social history under the double heading, system and lifeworld. As we have already seen, from a certain perspective, the term "modernity" signifies for Habermas a de-coupling of the social system, economy and state from the lifeworld, i.e., the ordinary world of lived experience. As social evolution becomes ever more complex, phenomena can be mediated either communicatively or instrumentally, i.e., either through the lifeworld or, under the imperatives of the system, through the media of money and power. In that process, the lifeworld, through which culture, society, and personality are mediated, can either be expanded or colonized.

Habermas coined the phrase "colonization of the lifeworld" to show how areas of social life can be subject to new forms of domination and control under the rubrics of an instrumental, rather than a communicative, rationality. In the context of law, when one wishes to look at the development of modern society from the process of juridification, one has the option of either colonization or, following the final statement of *The Tanner Lectures*, the democratization of the lifeworld. However, as areas of the lifeworld which are communicatively structured are taken over by the imperatives of the system, the tool which enables this process to go forward can be said to be juridification.

According to Habermas, using Kirchheimer's notion of the term, there were four waves of juridification characterizing the bourgeois state, the constitutional state, the democratic constitutional state, and the welfare state, respectively. In the original form, the Hobbesian state, the new subsystems of economy and state "extract what they need" from the "unspecific reservoir" of the lifeworld. This sets the pattern for subsequent modes of juridification. Even though new freedoms are granted, such as universal suffrage and the right to organize political parties in the democratic constitutional state, juridification erodes lifeworld structures to which it assumes a parasitic position. This is particularly true in the welfare state where the state has the good intention of promoting social integration through juridification. A certain "disintegration of life relations occurs

---

[25] The discussion of juridification (*Verrechtlichung*) documents the final and certainly one of the most important claims of the second volume of *The Theory of Communicative Action*, namely, that with the development of modern societies there is a tendency to colonize lifeworld experience. The proliferation of law in modern society illustrates how areas left to customary modes of organization are taken over by the modern state through processes of legalization.

when these are separated through legalized social intervention, from the consensual mechanisms that coordinate action and are transferred over to media like money and power."[26] The problem becomes one of law assuming the role of a steering medium which, through its intervention into the lifeworld, robs modern life of its consensual component.

If one studies the paradoxical structure of juridification in such areas as the family, the schools, social welfare policy, and the like, the meaning of the demands that regularly result from these analyses is easy to decipher. The point is to protect areas of life that are functionally dependent on social integration through values, norms and consensus formation, to preserve them from falling prey to the systematic imperatives of economic and administrative subsystems growing with dynamics of their own, and to defend them from becoming converted over, through the steering medium of the law, to a principle of association which is, for them, dysfunctional.[27]

By combining the discussion of law and morality with that of juridification we might conclude that in modernity, law, originally part of social life, became separated out under the imperatives of the system, to play the very ambiguous role of simultaneously eroding lifeworld structures while providing an anchor for new found freedoms.[28] Hence, although it might appear, as it indeed did to Max Weber, that law in modern society played an increasing autonomous role, in actuality law, which requires the lifeworld for its legitimation, is indeed dependent upon those very structures of communication which, under the imperatives of the steering mechanism, it attempts to mask. Hence, contrary to Weber, "There is no autonomous law without the realization of democracy."

To summarize, one might state that Habermas has chosen essentially two ways of dealing with the question of the law, one stemming from the distinction between system and lifeworld as presented in the theory of communicative action. In that context the debate over juridification illustrates the case for the colonization of the lifeworld. The discussion of law and morality, the other way of dealing with the question of the law, follows the fundamental themes of the discourse ethic which finds the link between law and morality in the discovery of certain procedures which provide the

[26] Habermas, *The Theory of Communicative Action*, vol. 2, p. 516.

[27] Ibid., p. 553.

[28] I realize that I am taking a somewhat more positive stand on juridification than Habermas does in the second volume of *The Theory of Communicative Action*. My hermeneutic assumption is the following: if one is to correlate the reading of juridification with the position developed in *The Tanner Lectures*, it would follow that juridification would have its positive as well as its negative meaning. In that sense, juridification would point beyond itself to the underlying link between law and morality which, in the context of instrumental reason, would remain undisclosed.

background for law. One could claim as a consequence of that discussion that, against legal positivism, this tie between law and morality can be re-established *contra* Weber and contemporary forms of legal positivism. In the next section I will examine Habermas's argument by presenting it as an alternative to two forms of critical legal theory, presented by Roberto Unger and Duncan Kennedy, who use the indeterminacy thesis in different ways to undermine any association between law and morality.

IV Critique of Objectivism and Formalism

No doubt the critique of objectivism and formalism is analogous to that of legal formalism which characterizes Max Weber's analysis of law.[29] Formalism implies strict adherence to rules and procedures which are justified on the basis of a certain view of the way things are, a view which is supposed to be *objective*, or, according to those indulging in both legal practice and legal theory, *true*. If it were only that simple. If there were only one version of formalism, if there were only one perspective on the objectivism to which the law referred for its legitimization. It is Unger's claim that the references are legion.[30] Hence, one can say that both formalism and objectivism rely on no one single formula, theory, or set of practices; rather, reference is multiple. The result is that the foundation of law is said to be contradictory and, therefore, false. The task of Roberto Unger in particular and of Critical Legal Studies in general has been to make manifest the contradictions within the law. Indeed, there is no recourse from the set of dilemmas made manifest by this exposé. Hence, the argument that, if we take the case of the practical jurist or lawyer, since there is no coherent body of legal doctrine available, decisions in law tend to be made on an *ad hoc* basis or, to put it bluntly, legal decisions are quickly instrumentalized, rationalized according to the arbitrary interest of legal professionals.

According to Unger, if one were to apply this insight to contemporary schools of law, the dilemmas of objectivism and formalism can be made

[29] There is some discussion of the precise relationship of the Critical Legal Studies movement to legal formalism and legal positivism, which saw their heyday at the turn of the century and later. The critique outlined by the Critical Legal Studies movement was anticipated by legal realism. However, one must conclude that legal realism never succeeded in undermining legal formalism. Hence, the analogy to Weber's critique is more than accidental.

[30] Here, I am anticipating the critique made by Roberto Unger in his monograph *The Critical Legal Studies Movement* (Cambridge, MA, Harvard University Press, 1983). Although I will concentrate on this text, Unger's more constructive and prophetic work is in *Law and Modern Society* (New York, The Free Press, 1975) and *Knowledge and Politics* (New York, The Free Press, 1976). I also consulted his current works on social theory and politics in manuscript form.

readily apparent. In the case of the so-called Law and Economics school, "an abstract market idea is identified with a specific version of the market . . . with all its surrounding social assumptions, real or imagined."[31] Inasmuch as it can be shown to be the case that this is one assumption among many which compete for attention among contemporary ideas about social theory, the very relativity of this form of "objectivism" is exposed. The claims of the Rights and Principles school can be similarly undermined. "It claims to discern in the leading ideas of the different branches of law, especially when illuminated by a scrupulous, benevolent, and well-prepared professional elite, the signs of an underlying moral order that can serve as the basis for a system of more or less natural rights."[32] This school is said to alternate between two options: one assumes that there is a "moral consensus" for legal theory, while the other maintains that "dominant legal principles count as manifestations of a transcendent moral order."[33]

There is a third position which mediates between the previous two, involving a number of diverse strategies. One position minimizes the extent to which law incorporates "conflict over desirable forms of human association"; another assumes that dominant legal ideas express higher moral insight; the third strategy is to generalize moral truth from particular legal doctrines, a strategy which is characterized by a method of hypostatization.

One might call this the relativist exposé; the discovery that there is no fundamental foundation upon which legal theory rests, that each attempt to connect it with some higher aim, some foundation beyond the generation itself, some concept of morality, some concept of economic utilitarianism, falters on the very pluralism of competing concepts of law and competing concepts of society. Unger claims that in both the Rights and Principles, and the Law and Economics schools we see the enterprise of "nineteenth-century legal science," to be sure in a somewhat "watered down" state. This endeavor, in turn, presumed a "version of the more common, conservative social doctrines that preceded the emergence of modern social theory."[34] What presumably exists behind these theories is a certain reliance on an assumed "natural form of society," with its attendant anthropological assumptions providing the fundamental, but unjustifiable, ingredient from which legal theory must be exorcized.

The dual task of critique and construction must spring from this insight. On the one hand, a revelatory emphasis upon the deep commitments of legal theory to social and naturalistic assumptions will expose these ideas for what they are, remnants of a metaphysical universe which we, as late

---

[31] Roberto Unger, *The Critical Legal Studies Movement*, p. 12.
[32] Ibid., p. 13.
[33] Ibid.
[34] Ibid., p. 14.

twentieth-century human beings, no longer habituate. On the other hand, if we are to experience freedom from the falsities of legal theory and practice, Unger must construct the kind of social and anthropological theory which compels our allegiance.

Unger does this by the construction of "deviationist doctrine," a methodology which is simultaneously critical and constructive, incorporating a number of strategies. Essentially, there are two models of deviationist doctrine, horizontal and vertical, each following distinct procedures. The first model, the horizontal version, begins with a concrete examination of a particular branch of law. It exposes undisclosed assumptions implicit in that particular area. Subsequently, it considers alternative forms of social life which can be "independently justified." "Finally, the model shows how this programmatic conception can serve as a regulative ideal for the development of current doctrine."[35] In other words, the task of critique leads to the construction of counter-factual theories, which presumably offer alternatives to current understanding. The second model, the vertical, works somewhat differently by conceiving the fields of law as expressions of principles and counter principles, which can be shown to be "contradictory." "The counter-vision, worked out through the analysis of these foci of controversy, brings a changed understanding of the relation between counter principles and principles."[36] After this it may be integrated into a larger view of legal theory resulting in the explication of "larger justifications and implications."[37]

Both models work from the empirical to the normative, from "authoritive rules and precedents," to "organizing principles and counter principles," to "imaginative schemes of social life that assign distinct models of human association to different sectors of social practice."[38] Both models expose inconsistencies and conflicts that exist at various levels. "Conventional legal doctrine, and the legal theories that propose to refine it the better to support it, try to suppress or minimize both the horizontal and vertical conflicts." Deviationist doctrine, on the contrary, attempts to bring these instabilities to the surface: "first, because this is the form subversion takes in the domain of legal ideas, and second, because if insight and justification can be achieved at all in legal doctrine or any other field of *normative argument*, they can be achieved only through the repeated practice of such subversion, under its double aspect of *internal development and visionary thought*."[39] One concludes that "deviationist doctrine" leads to an exposure

---

[35] Ibid., p. 88.
[36] Ibid.
[37] Ibid., p. 89.
[38] Ibid.
[39] Ibid. (Emphasis mine.)

and contiguous repudiation of the market and democracy. And having repudiated these assumptions, the position relies upon "visionary thought" to provide the alternatives found so sorely wanting in the contemporary world.

Ultimately, Unger, having repudiated law, turns toward the "visionary" side of his endeavor, the reconstruction of social theory. Here he takes the idea of society as artifact, and "pushes it to the hilt" in order to work out a totally contingent view of society. Central to this is an idea of "radically anti-naturalistic social theory" which undermines other modern forms of social theory which still have within them elements of a natural view of the origin and development of society. Implicit within Unger's perspective is the critique of "false necessity," the idea that certain characteristics of society have some necessary basis and foundation.

This later work on social theory may seem distant from earlier preoccupations with the law, inasmuch as a consideration of law is almost completely absent from the later work. However, it is not difficult to understand why Unger has embarked on this ambitious project of rethinking social theory. Having more or less repudiated law as a relativistic project evolving as a rationalization of disguised motivations of interested parties whose rationality was totally arbitrary, it is necessary to find, in fields independent of law, some justification for normative categories under which positions on the law may be adjudicated.

V   The Debate about Normativity

If we were to conceive of a kind of debate between Habermas's legal theory and Critical Legal Studies as represented by Unger, we could imagine the subject of that debate centering on the derivation of norms. We need only to be reminded that on the Habermasian side the task was to seek in legal theory its original relation to morality in the moment of indisponibility, which was indeed obscured by various forms of legal formalism and therefore misunderstood by Weber, but there nonetheless. Hence, procedures regarding justification associated with the original formulation of the social contract, while appearing to be instrumental, in fact contain that undisclosed remnant of an association between law and morality, which might be redeemed by an investigation into the characteristics of a procedural rationality which has its foundation in the modern development of practical reason. It is possible, then, to arrive at a conclusion regarding normativity and the law. Inasmuch as the rational kernel in the historical development of the law can be found in the discovery of certain procedures, one can suggest the road which the law must follow in order to be redeemed from formalism and instrumental association suggested by that alliance. Indeed, the processes of juridification may appear to be mainly systemic, and therefore purely instrumental and arbitrary, yet within that modern process a minimum form of rationality must be found.

No doubt Unger's response to this relatively detailed program would be both skeptical and critical, inasmuch as his argument relies on the observation that there is *no* rational element in the procedural adjudication of legal processes. Because, as "deviationist doctrine" can demonstrate, there is no method of justification which yields a determinate procedure, there is no immanent moral rationality upon which legal thought and process may rest its case. In fact, if we follow the procedures of deviationist doctrine, we will end up with the exposure of a series of direct and distinct contradictions. One might conclude that legal reasoning is nothing other than a form of political rhetoric.

As such, arguments over the nature of law are nothing other than ideological disputes which must be exposed by the deviationist methodology Unger has proposed. Unger, presumably, would want to unmask the Habermasian program as hopelessly naive, finding a form of rationality where only politics and ideology exist. But Unger is not a total deconstructionist. He definitely relates his understanding of the law to a form of normativity, which one may only assume arises from the "visionary" side of his enterprise. Here, Habermas would find Unger to be a kind of unreconstructed utopian inasmuch as there is no empirical foundation, no scientific basis, on which such an enterprise can proceed. Hence, the great contradiction arises in Unger's version of Critical Legal Studies: having so radically criticized all law as without foundation, how will it be possible to distinguish a version of social theory from which legal theory and practice can be extricated as anything other than politics and ideology?

VI The Case of Legal Formality

The same issue, the relationship of law and morality, can be taken up in another way and specified further by reference to an argument against legal formality by Duncan Kennedy.[40] Kennedy's purpose "is to clarify that

[40] By introducing this early argument from Kennedy, I am not attempting to identify Kennedy's position with that of Unger. Since Critical Legal Studies is in its second decade of development, there are now a variety of positions in the movement. Kennedy's position is much more skeptical than Unger's. His argument agrees with Unger's on the critical side, but it does not follow Unger's prophetic or visionary approach to the development of law and social theory. Kennedy, if anything, would want to see law as an instrument of social policy. My reason for choosing this particular argument from him is that it allows me to illustrate a classic procedure of the Critical Legal Studies school. That, in turn, will allow me to be more concrete about representative positions.

version of the liberal theory of justice which asserts that justice consists in
the impartial application of rules deriving their legitimacy from the prior
consent of those subject to them."[41] By raising the question of legal
formality in this way, one raises the question of the precise relationship
between the legislature which makes the rules in the democratic legal state,
and the judge who applies them. Legal formality, under the conditions of
the liberal contractarian state, assumes that a judge can legitimately conceive of himself or herself as the rule applier, one who can exercise the
application of rules in cases presented by disputing parties. This process,
the derivation and application of rules, is the embodiment of "formal," as
opposed to "substantive," rationality, by which the modern state can eliminate conflict. The rules are said to be arrived at through a process of
legislative mediation of "substantive-rational" interests. However, the assumption is that, once arrived at, they can be formally applied. Kennedy
makes the case that rules, when applied, lose their claim to be just,
inasmuch as they are derived from that which the legislature can provide,
merely, an "acceptable compromise." In turn, the duty to submit to the rule
is not derived from its inherent content as just, which it is not, but merely
from its legitimacy derived from the body of rules as a whole. Hence, the
following conclusion is possible: "The process of rule application itself has
nothing to do with 'justice' or 'right.'"[42] It does have to do with the
implementation of the interests of the state, which has derived the rules,
and the autonomy of the individual, who, under that system of rules, is
granted and guaranteed autonomy. Rules and adherence thereto not only
add to the autonomy of the individual, they restrain autonomy in order to
prevent harm to others. One should add that, although derivation of rules,
which are the result of a compromise and are neither just in their derivation
nor in their application, the category under which the rules are conceived
and under which the judge applies the rules is distributive justice. The idea
behind the application of the rule is that distributive justice, which has
been attended to in the legislature's working out of the rule, can be applied
mechanically through the application of the rule.

So much for legal formality in theory; in practice the case is somewhat
different. In actual litigation, rules which are the result of compromise are,
in fact, tested. The rule represents a kind of original agreement. The
judge's problem will be to apply this compromise to a situation in which
there again emerge conflicting interests. The litigant, on whom the rule, if
applied, would have an adverse effect, will attempt to persuade the judge to
dispense with the rule. "The litigant thus appears to be proposing that the

---

[41] Duncan Kennedy, "Legal Formality," *The Journal of Legal Studies*, vol. 2, (1973), p. 370.
[42] Ibid., p. 370.

judge forsake the secure and stable occupation of rule application for the obviously dangerous job of substantively rational arbiter of disputes about a constantly changing pattern of distributive justice and injustice." One could wait, of course, for the legislature to develop new rules for changing circumstances, which is, in fact what occurs in a changing world; but that really doesn't resolve the dilemma existing between the formulation of the rule and its application. The judge, in the process of application, has to move beyond the realm of legal formality in one way or another given the discrepancy between rule and application. In Kennedy's view, this raises a "moral" objection. "The judge cannot claim that legislative acquiescence legitimizes his [or her] action because he himself creates, through his decision of particular cases, the situation which will emerge in an as yet indeterminate constellation of legislative power."[43]

If one paused for a moment to reflect on this critique of legal formality based on the distinction between legislative rule construction and judicial rule application, one could find a fundamental similarity between the critical procedures developed by Habermas and Critical Legal Studies respectively. The fundamental flaw in legal formality is that it cannot restrict itself to its own narrowly formal definition. Hence, the judge, in the application of the rule, must reach beyond the realm of the given rule in light of the present situation in order to make a judgment which, one could surmise, has a substantively rational character. For both positions, this practical dilemma points to the fatal flaw in legal formalism. The Habermasian claim might be that this is precisely an instance of the case where the link between law and morality, which formalism had fought so valiantly to sever, is to be established. Critical Legal Studies eventually claims that the indeterminacy thesis regarding law can be established with this example. However, the real difference that separates the positions also derives from this example. Critical Legal Studies will *not* make the claim that this practical instance provides an illustration for joining law and morality. This should instead be taken as another instance of the arbitrariness of the law.

Allow me to return to Kennedy's argument. "The flaw in the logic of formality" is derived from this peculiar ambiguity in rule application: "The rule applied both implements the compromise by which the community legitimately disposes the problem of distributive justice, and provides a highly certain framework for private maximizing activity."[44] This is taken to mean that the possibility is created that "the rules will overthrow rather than execute the original compromise." This, in turn, makes it possible for the judge to "at least *consider* the possibility that he should disregard the

[43] Ibid., p. 385.
[44] Ibid., p. 387.

rule and examine the question of distributive justice."[45] Equally, the judge could attempt to "return to formal rule application with the single purpose of securing the certainty of the framework for private maximizing."[46] In other words, theoretically the judge could return to the legislature. But this possibility is only theoretical inasmuch as, according to Kennedy's definition of the rule as a representation of compromise, it already has a certain ambiguity written into it when made the basis for a practical decision. Hence, appeal to the legislature is no sure resolution. If the rule appears unfair to the judge, "Loyalty to the rule is a decision for a particular political outcome; disregard of the rule threatens the very mechanism of order through compromise."[47] So one concludes that the application of the rule is a kind of roulette game in which the judge is damned if she does and dammed if she doesn't. "*All* laws are gambling contracts, as Hobbes saw long ago. *All* laws pose to the judge and litigant the question whether they should accept a concept of the administration of justice as a mechanism for the collection of resulting debts. It makes no sense to expect that yet one more gamble − a gamble on gambling − will make the problem go away."[48]

To summarize Kennedy's position, the ambiguity arising between the legislative generation of rules and their judicial application suggests that, in the case of judicial application, the judge has a series of alternatives which are equally available to her. She can attempt to rely on pure formalism. This may not work and probably will not work, but it will not prevent her from attempting to do so. She can dispense with the rule altogether and decide directly on the merits of the case. She can work out some compromise, which is more likely to be the case, between extreme formalism at one end of the spectrum and reliance on substantively rational issues on the other. I should like to derive two hypothetical readings from this position, one favoring Critical Legal Studies, the other Habermas's interpretation.

In the first reading, since the judge has at her disposal a series of alternatives, none of which is a necessary one, her decision is likely to be arbitrary, the consequence of a series of irrational variables which happen to affect her decision. If this is the case, there is really no difference between law and ideology, law and politics. Further, if there is to be an association between law and morality, it would be necessary to develop a theory of law from an entirely different perspective (Unger's alternative).

In the second reading, the one inspired by Habermas, the series of

[45] Ibid.
[46] Ibid., p. 388.
[47] Ibid., p. 389.
[48] Ibid.

alternatives available to the judge would be seen as anything but arbitrary. One could develop the kind of thesis which suggests that the attempt to adhere to principles of legal formality breaks the bonds of legal formality, leading to the introduction of issues of moral-practical procedural rationality. Here, when the judge attempts to apply the formal rule, although the practical circumstance of litigation forces a re-definition of the rule to meet the practical situation, the procedure which guarantees the effectiveness of the rule applied finds its origin in moral-practical rationality. This context would demonstrate the point that questions of morality are associated with the problem of justification, while the proper realm of law is that of application. However, in the procedural application of the rule, law and morality come together.

VII The Case Against Legal Positivism

Habermas's technique, as we have seen, attempts to overcome the positivistic dissociation between law and morality by dissociating questions of justification from those of application by a reconstructive procedure which clearly distinguishes normative from descriptive statements. Through the process of procedural reconstruction, Habermas claims to be able, through a moment of idealization, to separate normative from descriptive assumptions and adjudicate the moral presuppositions implicit in legal theory and practice vis-à-vis the conditions of ideal speech and with implicit assumptions about communication. The claim is that rationality implicit in legal procedure demonstrates that link between law and morality.

In so doing, Habermas has achieved two things. First, by treating the question of law and morality in this way it would appear that one has broken through the barrier erected around the law by legal positivism, the barrier that separated law from morality. Second, it would appear that Habermas has avoided resting his case for the link between law and morality on the basis of the development of law in modern liberal societies. True to his definition of the project of modernity, he has limited his case to procedures of rationality alone. In other words, he has sustained the position, referred to in the last chapter, of suspicion regarding culture and tradition as the basis from which one can generate an argument for morality. As I have suggested before, it is clear why he does this. If the link between law and morality were to be approached from the inside, as it were, from a purely interpretative position, one would run the risk of resting one's case on a potentially bad culture or tradition. In the terminology of law, how does one get good laws out of a bad society? For example, it would appear that, if one argued that the link between law and morality were given within a culture or tradition, then potentially bad societies – Germany under National Socialism, South Africa with its system of apartheid – would provide precisely the example of that mode. Hence, by basing the case on procedures of universalization, one is able to avoid these problems.

But can one really do this? Can one establish the link between law and morality in a non-contextual manner? Can one get beyond the legal context? I will examine this question by considering the link between law and morality on interpretative grounds, an argument which I take to be essentially contextualist in character. Roland Dworkin[49] puts forward such an interpretative argument which I will use for the purposes of linking law and morality, highlighting integrity as a quasi-Platonic, Protestant virtue granted to interpreters of the law.[50] In contrast to Habermas, Dworkin makes two assumptions about interpretation. First, in legal texts, one cannot distinguish between the descriptive and the normative.[51] Second, that which grants a certain normativity to interpretation has to do with the history of interpretation.[52] The former assumption leads to the proposition that equity is built into the structure of law, while the latter assumes that beyond positivist historical interpretation there is a certain obsession with history that characterizes the institution of legal interpretation, embodied in the person who judges, which goes beyond legal positivism. In other words, it is the one who judges who is characterized as having a certain political virtue, integrity, which is demonstrated in the legal process. The notion of integrity is supplemented by two further assumptions granted to the theory of interpretation as such. In what is often said to be the chaotic body of legal doctrine, the interpreter seeks a coherent account. As such, the task of the interpreter is to bring order out of chaos. Beyond that, the interpreter will seek to achieve the best interpretation.

Dworkin's argument, which I have used for my purposes as one for the link between law and morality, presents a peculiar challenge to the Habermasian attempt to connect these two realms. If it is the case that the distinction between the normative and the descriptive is already linked within the legal text itself, then processes of idealization which are perceived to be essential to the task of linking law and morality by Habermas are unnecessary. In other words, the principle of equity, which is granted in

---

[49] Roland Dworkin, *Law's Empire* (Cambridge MA, Harvard University Press, 1986).

[50] Dworkin has developed a practical argument which attempts, on the basis of a hermeneutic theory of interpretation, to link law and morality in relationship to the practice of interpretation.

[51] Dworkin would find normative implications in any descriptive statement.

[52] It follows that Dworkin's agreement is essentially a contextualist one which finds idealization both impossible and unnecessary.

Habermas's view by the procedures of idealization, is already given within the law. If that were the case, there would be no need to separate justification from application. Beyond that, Dworkin would see no need for the postulation of the ideal communication community. Legal opinions do not necessarily presuppose an ideal consensus. It is in this sense that Dworkin's theory is a Protestant theory. Further, the political virtue, integrity, as perceived in the process of legal interpretation, with the associated assumptions regarding the coherence of legal doctrine and the best interpretation, would simply buttress this criticism. It is not in the idealized, but rather in the actual process of legal interpretation that the link between law and morality is granted.

6

Reading Habermas: Modernity vs Postmodernity

I Questions

I have argued throughout this book that there is a certain coherence to Habermas's work. If one took the appendix to *Knowledge and Human Interests* as paradigmatic, it is clear that, from this point on, Habermas has attempted more or less to change the conditions for the legitimation of what he called "knowledge-constitutive interests," one of which was "emancipatory."[1] This was Habermas the sociologist buying into a quasi-Kantian philosophical program which placed "epistemology" at the fore-front of the argument. It is interesting to look back to see that it was "critical social science" which was designated as the bearer of this task. One can begin to reconstruct the later development. Even then it was clear that a purely transcendental program of justification was suspect. The metaphor "quasi-transcendental" suggests this. He was at that time, as he has always been, at least partially convinced by the work of Karl-Otto Apel. But Habermas has also always been the social scientist who respects empirical evidence. The argument for the transcendental grounding of norms and truth claims is, when taken alone, too abstract, too purely philosophical for him.

The two poles, between which Habermas's work has been suspended since the mid-sixties, are the transcendental and the empirical. In becoming a philosopher, Habermas never stopped being a social scientist. As we have seen, Rorty's criticism of the view presented in *Knowledge and Human Interests* was simply that Habermas, in attempting to ground the claims of critical theory, works in the shadow of the "Kantian grid" and divides the domains of knowledge into a tripartite structure. The clue to the criticism is present in the title of Rorty's book, *Philosophy and the Mirror of Nature*. From Rorty's point of view, Habermas represents one more attempt to use philosophy as a way to image nature. Did Habermas, with the publication of *The Theory of Communicative Action* change direction or did he sustain the

[1] Richard Bernstein has written an excellent analysis of the transition from *Knowledge and Human Interests* to *The Theory of Communicative Action* in *Habermas and Modernity*, ed. Richard Bernstein (Cambridge, Polity Press, 1985).

program of the sixties in an expanded and reconstructed form? In a sense, he did both. There is a kind of tenaciousness in Habermas's work. The transcendental-empirical polarity that existed earlier has been retained to a certain extent, but the program has been reformulated to meet both the demands of criticism and the changed philosophical situation.

In this sense, the key text in the later development of Habermas's work is "Philosophy as Stand-in and Interpreter," which was conceived as an answer to Rorty. Here Habermas suggests a distinctive role for philosophy as the stand-in for science. In some ways, this may appear as an odd and unusual text. What do philosophy and science have to do with each other except as philosophy of science? But this is not philosophy of science. Instead, and this is what is really new in the Habermasian program of recent years, philosophy relates itself to science as reconstructive science. The transcendental and the empirical exist as boundaries between which the project of reconstructive science emerges.

Does this mean that the claim to redeem the unfinished project of modernity, the metaphor that I have liked best as a way of capturing the meaning of Habermas's recent work, rests on the results of reconstructive science? Has Habermas shifted his attempt to ground his project from the quasi-transcendental to the quasi-empirical? At times, Habermas seems to answer the question in the affirmative. If the claims of reconstructive science are based on empirical evidence, and if that evidence changes through the results of further research, it appears that the claims of reconstructive science also have to change. Scientific evidence, in whatever form, is always fallible. Certainly, Habermas formulates this side of his project not only to meet the criticisms of Rorty, but also to meet those of Karl-Otto Apel, who sustains the enterprise of transcendental philosophy in its purest contemporary form. In his own terms, Apel is rightfully suspicious of the project of reconstructive science.

But there is a larger question here. Can (or, better, should) the unfinished project of modernity rest on the claims of reconstructive science? Isn't there a conceptual confusion here? Does Habermas mean that the unfinished project of modernity, with its "emancipatory" potential, can be falsified if the claims of reconstructive science are falsified?

The Theory of Communicative Action represented Habermas's most massive attempt to overcome the dilemma resulting from the program of epistemologically grounding the claims of emancipation. To achieve this objective, he turned to the philosophy of language. In the second and third chapters of this book I illustrated how individual this attempt was. Looking back, it was as if one could build into language the epistemological, emancipatory claims of the earlier period. That is no easy task. It could only be done by bringing in Karl-Otto Apel's program of the philosophy of language as first philosophy, which rests on the fundamental assumption that the development of language is isomorphic with the development of communities. Hence, one could understand why, from this perspective, emancipatory potentials are built within the very structure of language. The theory of language, then, taken from a reconstruction of speech-act theory and conceived of as a theory of rationality, with its implicit distinction between the perlocutionary and the illocutionary (code words for the instrumental and the emancipatory), allowed for the reconstruction of social theory *vis-à-vis* a kind of immanent critique. This means that Weber, Lukács, Horkheimer, and Adorno could all be perceived as imprisoned in dilemmas of a philosophy of consciousness confined to the expressions of instrumental reason. At this point, my original suspicion, raised in the first chapter, began to manifest itself. There was a certain uneasy tension between the project of modernity and the philosophy of language which was supposed to redeem it. It was as if language could be conceived as in some way containing within it the unfinished project of modernity. I used this criticism to begin to make the point. The project of modernity is a noble ideal. If conceived as a project of emancipation, as liberation from oppression, as the means of overcoming hidden, latent forms of domination, I am in agreement. But can it really be completed with this conception of the philosophy of language?

In the second half of the third chapter, I probed this dilemma further by entering into the discussion of the distinction between system and lifeworld. Reformulated in terms of this version of the philosophy of language, it appears that system imperatives are instrumental while those of the lifeworld are communicative. Here one encounters the most peculiar interpretive dilemma. Habermas insists on a distinction which seems to rob the emancipatory thesis of its potential force; to be sure, an idealization from which the "colonization of the lifeworld" thesis is derived, but at what price? Is it that once we know the illocutionary has a certain priority over the perlocutionary in language we will struggle to make this the case in society? Or is it that only through the tasks of reconstruction that we can make room for the old claim that emancipation will triumph, but this time under the guise of reconstructive science?

In the domain of discourse ethics and legal theory, the situation is somehow clearer. Here Habermas makes his claims regarding the project of emancipation in a more nuanced way. But a new enemy appears, an enemy, to be sure, pre-figured in the critiques of Weber, Lukács, Adorno, and Horkheimer, but new just the same: contextualism. For the critic, the question arises, what would the Habermasian project come to if it were not for the enterprise of reconstructive science? Suspended between the poles of the transcendental and the empirical, discourse ethics is seen as a kind of "privileged access" to the theory of moral development. Science, as reconstructive science, can document the emancipatory claims of the project of modernity. But what is this reconstructive science? Is it really anything other than certain constructs taken from interpretations of moral assumptions implicit in the historical development of democratic societies? In other words, is reconstructive science itself contextualist? Here one understands how close Habermas comes to contextualism.

One therefore poses the dilemma more radically. Without reconstructive science, Habermas would have to argue either on a purely transcendental basis as Apel does, or he would have to accede to the contextualists. In other words, without reconstructive science, discourse ethics has to be argued on a contextualist basis. But, as we have seen, Habermas resists this move. Since the debates with Gadamer in the sixties, Habermas has been suspicious of a purely interpretative, hermeneutic position. Consequently, Habermas has attempted to get beyond the relativistic implications of hermeneutics by arguing for a theory of rationality which is not limited to or contained by a specific tradition. In the more recent period of Habermas's writing, this has led to an argument for a kind of moral universalism contained in a consensus theory of truth and normative validity which can sustain universalist claims on the basis of the argumentative assumptions built into the theory of rationality itself. I tend to see this as more or less separate from reconstructive science, correlative to, but not identical with, Karl-Otto Apel's slightly more transcendental approach to discourse ethics. The transcendental-empirical polarity remains.

As suggested earlier, I suspect the clue to this move in the recent development of Habermas's work is biographical. Habermas was fifteen at the end of the Second World War. As a student, he read Heidegger enthusiastically. Slowly, during those post-war years in Germany, the truth of the past began to reveal itself. The shock of recognition, the sense of betrayal, register in almost everything Habermas has written. His argument for moral universalism against contextualism is an argument that attempts to rest the very narrow claims of morality on the basis of rationality alone. The almost Husserlian obsession for grounding those claims emerges here.

But there are tough arguments against the claims of moral universalism. Can questions of morality be separated from questions of the good life? The neo-Aristotelians say no. Habermas's arguments against Aristotelian teleology and metaphysics are convincing ones. The one which denies the separation of the virtual from the actual is somehow more telling and more difficult to defeat. It suggests that the idealization implicit in the argument for moral universalism is not only unnecessary, but also impossible. But, if unnecessary, the argument for moral universalism is only another contextualist one. Habermas has fought this critique and, from his point of view, for good reason. To give in to the critiques of moral universalism is to accede to the relativist and potentially corrupt implications of a contextualist, interpretative position. Hence, as I suggested earlier, Habermas will attempt to strengthen the claims of moral universalism rather than accede to his contextualist critics. But again, at what price?

The other, equally difficult, argument against moral universalism is the one that questions whether or not this assertion is really based on language. Are the claims regarding communication, with the attendant assumptions regarding the ideal speech situation, assumptions which include egalitarian and non-dominating theses, really linguistic claims at all? The broad issue here is whether or not Habermas, as he turns toward moral theory, sticks to his overarching claim, first put forth in *The Theory of Communicative Action*, namely, to overcome the difficulties of the philosophy of consciousness with the insights of the philosophy of language. The charge is that assumptions developed to sustain the position on moral universalism are not really linguistic assumptions at all, but rather are derived from the history of voluntarism. There is a Lockian ring to this charge. When Locke, in his *A Letter Concerning Toleration*,[2] argues for separation of the private from the public sphere, the separation of religion from civil society, he argues that the aims and goals of Christian and non-Christian societies are essentially voluntary. Furthermore, John Stewart Mill, in *On Liberty*,[3] takes that argument almost into the public sphere. What could be more voluntaristic than the ideal communication society with no force other than the force of the better argument? It seems to me that, instead of through Kant, the link to Peirce and Mead is found here. Perhaps there is an outside chance of linking the theory of communication to a revised, formerly intentionalist semantic, speech-act theory; but this appears to be an extraordinarily difficult, perhaps unnecessary, route to take.

Turning toward the only partially developed philosophy of law, similar problems emerge. Here the strategy is somewhat different: to link law and morality against the positivistic claim that law has nothing to do with morality. Here, of course, one hears the echoes of a great tradition in legal and social philosophy, from Al-Farabi through Thomas, from Hobbes to Locke, from Kant to Hegel. The problem in Al-Farabi was, implicitly against Augustine, to simply link religion and society. With Thomas, it was to show how natural or divine law was linked to human law. Hobbes tried to develop a convincing, secular argument for moving from the state of nature to the state of society; the chief ingredient of that argument was an appeal to natural law. One might say that the natural law tradition died with

[2] John Locke, *A Letter Concerning Toleration* (Indianapolis, Bobbs-Merrill, 1950).

[3] John Stewart Mill, *On Liberty*, ed. Elizabeth Rapaport (Indianapolis, Hackett, 1978).

Hegel's critique of it,[4] but the problem remained: how, in a secular society, to link law and morality.

Habermas tried to redeem that link on the basis of certain eminently Kantian assumptions regarding the nature of rationality implicit in the procedures of argumentation. As the previous chapter illustrated, this argument works well against the skeptics. How will it work against the contextualists? Certainly, Aristotle's assumption that good societies have good laws won't work. It's too simple. What about bad societies? They have, or have had, laws too. Here it would appear that Habermas's attempt not only to separate questions of justification from application, but also to link law and morality on the basis of a procedural conception of rationality, establishes that link without falling into the dilemma faced by the contextualists. The solutions in law are foreshadowed by the solutions in moral theory. But the same dilemmas would follow. Certainly, Rorty's suggestion that the Anglo-American is somehow better than the German will not do.[5] But arguments which take the body of law as a whole, on an interpretative basis, are difficult to counter. This is difficult because the principles of equity can be discovered within the law itself and will be used as criteria against so-called bad societies. In other words, they link law and morality without requiring, in Habermas's terms, procedures of justification and the associated processes of idealization.

II The Reading

My purpose thus far has been to summarize the argument of the book; I have not quite completed the task. My initial argument was that there is a certain tension between the project of modernity and the philosophy of language, a thesis derived from the reading of *The Theory of Communicative Action* and *The Philosophical Discourse of Modernity*. I have chosen the metaphor, "the project of modernity," a project declared to be "unfinished," because of its graphic character. Throughout the book, I have tried to think through the "work" in the context of the "criticism." Now I want to return to a promise, left unfulfilled at the end of the first chapter, to take up Habermas's reading of the philosophical tradition precisely where I left it, at the point where, after the consideration of the tradition from Hegel to Nietzsche, he considers Heidegger, Foucault, and Derrida. What interests me here is not the truth or falsity, the rightness or wrongness of the

[4] G. W. F. Hegel, *Natural Law*, tr. T. M. Knox (Philadelphia, University of Pennsylvania Press, 1975).

[5] Richard Rorty, "Thugs and Theorists; A Reply to Bernstein," *Political Theory*, 15:4 (November, 1987), pp. 564–80.

interpretation, but simply trying to understand Habermas's reading. Much is at stake here. It has to do with what we Americans call "Continental philosophy." One might call it a battle for the academic soul of the Continental tradition.

The first chapter ended with a certain suspicion about the way Habermas reads the tradition, in other words, he is somehow much more comfortable with both the reading and the critique of Hegel than of Nietzsche. It was Habermas, after all, for whom Hegel set up the problematic of modernity, the problem of reconciling the potentially unmediated spheres of modernity which hover over his project "like a tangled mobile," on the basis of a concept of reason that generates itself out of itself. For Habermas, Nietzsche repudiated that tradition by attempting to get behind it. My guess is that the lingering third that remains unexplained in this encounter between Hegel and Nietzsche is Kant's third critique. Habermas, like Hegel, simply forces aesthetic rationality into the mold. For him, there will always be something unintelligible about a form of reason which does not fit with science and morality. Nietzsche represents that alternative.

(a) Heidegger

With Heidegger, the critical disciple of Nietzsche, the discourse becomes intense. Habermas's thesis, stated in a chapter heading, is that Heidegger undermines Western rationalism through the critique of metaphysics.[6] The correlate thesis is that, "In so doing he arrives at a temporalized philosophy of origins."[7] In some ways, Heidegger is the greatest challenge because, for Habermas, he is the one philosopher who most effectively undermines the normativity implied in the project of modernity. "No matter whether modern ideas make their entry in the name of reason or the destruction of reason, the prism of the modern understanding of Being refracts *all* normative orientations into the power claims of a subjectivity crazed with self-aggrandizement."[8] But for Habermas this undermining is an illusion. Heidegger engages in the destruction of the history of metaphysics. As Habermas sees it, there is a Hegelian parallel here. Whether one constructs, as in the case of Hegel, or de-structs, as in the case of Heidegger, there is a normative standard here. "To be sure, the critical reconstruction of metaphysics cannot get along without its *own* standard. This it borrows from the implicitly normative concept of the 'completion' of metaphysics."[9] Here the stage is set for the critique of Heidegger. The refrain is familiar

---

[6] Jürgen Habermas, *The Philosophical Discourse of Modernity*, tr. Fredrick Lawrence (Cambridge, MA, MIT Press, 1987), p. 131.

[7] Ibid.

[8] Ibid., p. 132.

[9] Ibid., p. 134.

but this time the stakes are higher: the very attempt to disengage oneself from the project of modernity implies the project of modernity. And from this assumption, which will be the most controversial of all, a distinctive consequence is derived: Heidegger partakes of the dilemmas of the philosophy of the subject.

Heidegger thinks in the shadow of Nietzsche. "The idea of the origin and end of metaphysics owes its critical potential to the circumstance that Heidegger moves about within the modern time-consciousness no less than Nietzsche."[10] But, of course, Heidegger, no less than Nietzsche, attempts to overcome modern time-consciousness by getting behind it. In this reading Heidegger doesn't succeed. "Just as Nietzsche once expected from Wagnerian opera a tiger's leap into the futural past of ancient Greek tragedy, so Heidegger would like to be transported by Nietzsche's metaphysics of the will to power back to the pre-Socratic origins of metaphysics."[11] This project, a project of thinking, which Nietzsche attempted to ground in art, Heidegger tries to ground in a thinking that goes beyond the conceptual, a thinking that is more "rigorous." Like Nietzsche, Heidegger abandons science. For Heidegger, who also belongs to those who would like to abandon the philosophy of the subject, science is enclosed within that very philosophy. For Habermas, Heidegger's appeal lies in the "special knowledge" of the "initiate".

Though Habermas riles against this quasi-religious appeal to the abolition of the philosophy of the subject, even he finds, if only on one occasion, an ally for the communication thesis. "Heidegger turns as always against the monological approach of the philosophy of consciousness, which takes as its point of departure the individual subject who in knowing and acting stands over against an objective world of things and occurrences."[12] Heidegger even highlights "mutual understanding." Referring to Heidegger's 1939 lectures on Nietzsche, Habermas quotes Heidegger: "Because misunderstanding and lack of understanding are only degenerate species of mutual understanding ... the approach of human beings toward one another in their self-sameness and selfhood has first to be grounded through mutual understanding."[13] But alas, "Heidegger believes that insights of *this kind* are exclusively reserved to his critique of metaphysics."[14] In other words, Heidegger does not have at hand the alternative resources that lead one out of the philosophy of the subject. "The philosophy of the subject is by no means an absolutely reifying power that imprisons all

[10] Ibid.
[11] Ibid.
[12] Ibid., p. 136.
[13] Ibid., p. 137.
[14] Ibid.

discursive thought and leaves open nothing but a flight into the immediacy of mystical ecstasy."[15] In other words, Heidegger chose one path out of the the philosophy of subject. Habermas's contention is that there are "*other* paths."

Reflecting for a moment, one might ask, could it be that Habermas is in agreement with Heidegger? Certainly, the task is to lead us out of the philosophy of the subject. Where is the disagreement? Only about the means? How close is Habermas to Heidegger, one wonders. At the very least, it is interesting that Habermas chooses to critique Heidegger on grounds that were established only on the basis of Heidegger's own thought. He states: "The fact that Heidegger sees, in the history of philosophy and the sciences after Hegel, nothing but a monotonous spelling out of the ontological pre-judgments (*Vor-Urteile*) of the philosophy of the subject can only be explained by the fact that, even in rejecting it, *he still remains caught in the problems of the subject in the form Husserlian phenomenology had presented to him.*"[16] One need only point out that this is the standard form of phenomenological critique, the parameters of which Heidegger first fixed in the introduction of *Being and Time.*[17] Suffice it to say that, throughout his later work Habermas has attempted to lead us out of the philosophy of the subject. My suspicion is that the overcoming of Heidegger will be the most Promethean of Habermas's attempts. One need only remember that Habermas began his philosophical apprenticeship by reading Heidegger. Thus, one might expect that here the program to redeem the project of modernity will find its most passionate defense.

As suggested, Habermas follows the procedure of standard phenomenological critique. His text is ripe with references to Husserl. Even in the "Letter on Humanism," which sums up the results of the Nietzsche interpretations of the previous decade, Heidegger cannot characterize his own procedure otherwise than through implicit reference to Husserl. He wants, as he puts it there, to "retain the essential help of the phenomenological way of seeing and dispense with the inappropriate concern with 'science' and 'research.'"[18] Heidegger never gives up on the "intuitionism" of Husserl's "procedure." "Husserl's way of *posing problems* also remains

---

[15] Ibid.

[16] Ibid. (Emphasis mine.)

[17] I use the phrase, "standard phenomenological critique" to designate the kind of critique of Husserl that came to be endorsed by the second and third generation of the phenomenological movement. Although Heidegger originated the critique, it need not be confined to him. Hence, it might be said that was the standard or commonly accepted way in which later phenomenology would look at the first generation of phenomenologists. To the extent that Habermas shares with Heidegger the diagnosis of the dilemma of philosophy as being confined to the philosophy of the subject, he endorses Heidegger's analysis.

[18] Ibid., p. 138.

normative for Heidegger, inasmuch as he merely turns the basic epistemo-logical question into an ontological one."[19] Even on the question of inter-subjectivity Heidegger remains a Husserlian. "In *Being and Time*, Heidegger does not construct intersubjectivity any different than Husserl does in the *Cartesian Meditations*: '*Dasein*' as in each case mine constitutes being-with in the same way that the transcendental ego constitutes the intersubjectivity of the world shared by myself and others."[20] And from this one can deduce the conclusion: "Heidegger passes beyond the horizon of the philosophy of consciousness only to stay in the shadows."[21]

Habermas uses the standard form of phenomenological critique to critique a position in phenomenology. This form of critique could be taken, as I have suggested, from a reading of Heidegger himself. In fact, a careful reading of Heidegger suggests that he realized later in life that he had been caught up in the very dilemma from which he was attempting to free himself.[22] The charge that Heidegger remained in the remnants of a framework of transcendental phenomenology could have been made by the later Heidegger against the earlier Heidegger. But this leads to the question: if Heidegger was aware of this, what is the meaning of the *Kehre*, the turning toward the later position? The question is twofold, associated with both the meaning, and various explanations of what led to the *Kehre*. It is precisely at this point that Habermas departs radically from standard phenomenological critique.

Habermas's thesis is by now well known.[23] Of course, one could read Heidegger's philosophy internally as an attempt to overcome the philosophy of the subject. The standard interpretation of the later Heidegger has followed this approach. The answers to the question are then posed from within the body of the work itself. They are obvious: either Heidegger did succeed or he did not. Even the consistent Heideggerian could answer the question either way. To be sure, the projects of Derrida and Foucault − one could add many others to the list − have followed this line of inter-pretation. Habermas's claim is more radical. *One cannot explain the 'Kehre'*

---

[19] Ibid.

[20] Ibid., p. 150.

[21] Ibid., p. 139.

[22] This appears to be the best explanation for the absence of the promised second volume of *Being and Time*.

[23] Apart from the discussion of Heidegger in *The Philosophical Discourse of Modernity*, Habermas has reiterated his position in an essay originally written as the foreword to the German edition of Victor Farias's book, *Heidegger et la Nazism* (1988) translated into English as "Work and Weltanschauung: The Heidegger Controversy from a German Perspective" in *The New Conservatism; Cultural Criticism and the Historians' Debate* (Cambridge, MA, MIT Press, 1989). While the latter text is a more distanced and scholarly analysis, the former is more passionate. I prefer the former.

without understanding Heidegger's involvement in and complicity with National Socialism.

The normative implications of this thesis have and will continue to descend upon the academic community like a reverberating firestorm which has yet to be contained. Searching for a metaphor, words such as "heart," "center," "apex" come to mind. At this point, one begins to understand what the Habermasian project is all about. We have arrived at the center of this reading of Habermas. For him, Heidegger descended from the lofty heights of a kind of mythic archaism into what must be seen as the most rank form of contextualism. Precisely here, Habermas's claims for moral universalism can be read as a kind of testament of one who says, *never again*.

How did Heidegger get out of the "dead end" of *Being and Time*? For Habermas there is, to be sure, an internal reading which answers the question. "Heidegger renounces the claim ascribed to metaphysics of self-grounding and ultimate grounding."[24] "Being," as an "event," can only be experienced "meditatively" and "presented narratively." "Heidegger rejects existential ontology's concept of freedom."[25] "Dasein" renounces its authorship of "world-projects"; the "enterprise of productivity" is given to "Being" itself. Beyond that, Heidegger negates the "foundationalism" that characterized philosophy from Kant through Husserl. For Habermas, this means that the "first principle of *Ursprungsphilosophie* is temporalized."[26] Implied in this process is the "historicization of Being."

In Habermas's view, this internal reading doesn't tell the story. The thesis is elaborated: "I suspect that Heidegger could find his way to the temporalized *Ursprungsphilosophie* of the later period only by way of his temporary identification with the National Socialist movement − to whose inner truth and greatness he still attested in 1935."[27] The framework for this interpretation is set by the now infamous "*Das Selbstbehauptung der Deutschen Universität. Das Rektorat 1933/34.*" The point is that the speech was written and given in the shadow of *Being and Time*, which "takes on the character of a project: the project of a new authentic form of life for the people."[28] The will of *Dasein* becomes identified with *Volk*. *Dasein's* will becomes the will of the people. Heidegger contextualized his philosophy. How would he decontextualize it? Habermas speculates that Heidegger could have renounced National Socialism. "A plain, political-moral re-valuation of National Socialism would have attacked the foundations of the

---

[24] Jürgen Habermas, *The Philosophical Discourse* of *Modernity*, p. 152.
[25] Ibid.
[26] Ibid., p. 153.
[27] Ibid., p. 155.
[28] Ibid., p. 158.

renewed ontology and called into question the entire theoretical approach."[29] Heidegger chose another route. His "disappointment with National Socialism" was "elevated beyond the foreground sphere of responsible judgment and action." It was "stylized into an objective error"; an error which "gradually revealed itself in history." In this way the "continuity" with *Being and Time* was not "endangered."

The moral tone of the critique is clear. Heidegger could have chosen another way out of the philosophy of the subject which, in a contextualized way, became part of the mission of National Socialism. He didn't. Instead, in this view, he constructed a kind of philosophy of omission which objectified and therefore eliminated *guilt* and *responsibility*. The text is ripe with moral indignation. "He interprets the untruth of the movement by which he had let himself be dragged along not in terms of an existential fallenness into the 'they' for which one is subjectively responsible, but as an objective withholding of the truth."[30] And then comes the judgment: "That the eyes of the most resolute philosopher were only gradually opened up to the nature of the regime — for this astoundingly delayed reading of world history — the course of the world is supposed to assume authorship, not concrete history, indeed, but a sublimated history promoted to the lofty heights of ontology." And finally, a last, terse, ironic comment sums up the entire interpretation of the later Heidegger: "Thus was born the concept of the history of Being."[31] Heidegger did not lead us out of the philosophy of the subject, he merely inverted it.

What can one say about this reading of Heidegger? Is it wrong? Is it an oversimplification? Should it be rejected because it is posed as an external reading? Fortunately, this book is about Habermas and not Heidegger. The questions will be answered and re-answered by others. My suspicion is that the reading is so powerful in its moral claim that it cannot be dismissed as just another reading of Heidegger. Lévi-Strauss, in his article on "The Structural Study of Myth,"[32] made the point with regard to the Oedipus myth that, along with the mythic, the dramatic, the historical readings of that myth, the more recent Freudian reading must be added. My point is quite simple: future readings of Heidegger will have to take this one into account. However, the reading poses ambiguities. Does it mean that others who have followed Heidegger by trying to find the path out of modernity are to be similarly charged? Is the way out of modernity the way out of guilt and responsibility?

[29] Ibid., p. 159.
[30] Ibid.
[31] Ibid.
[32] Claude Lévi-Strauss, "The Structural Study of Myth," *Journal of American Folklore*, LXXVIII: 270 (October/December, 1955), pp. 428–44.

(b) Derrida

Habermas reads Derrida in the shadow of his reading of Heidegger's concept of the history of Being. For Habermas, "Derrida's deconstructions faithfully follow the movement of Heidegger's thought."[33] This means that Derrida, like Heidegger and like Habermas himself, begins his analysis with what I have called standard phenomenological critique. One recalls that the "unfinished" project of modernity is to lead us out of the philosophy of the subject. Derrida learned, and at the same time transformed, structuralism. "He lays bare the inverted foundationalism of this thought by once again going beyond the ontological difference of Being to the difference proper to writing, which puts an origin, already set in motion, yet one level deeper."[34] In other words, Derrida's strategy, to move beyond the problem of "origins" by turning to writing, only displaces the problem of origins to a deeper level. The problem remains. Habermas remains unconvinced. "The advantage that Derrida may have hoped to gain from grammatology and an apparent concretizing/textualizing of the history of being *remains insignificant*."[35] Hence, the conclusion: "As a participant in the philosophical discourse of modernity, Derrida inherits the weakness of a critique of metaphysics that does not shake loose of the intentions of first philosophy."[36]

Habermas could have chosen to end the reading of Derrida at that point. He doesn't. Again, as in the case of Heidegger, the text reverberates with moral indignation. "Despite his transformed gestures, in the end he, too, promotes only a mystification of palpable social pathologies; he, too, disconnects essential (namely, deconstructive) thinking from scientific analysis; and he, too, lands at an empty, formula-like avowal of some indeterminate authority."[37] To be sure, in this reading there is some slight distancing of Derrida from Heidegger. The indeterminate authority has shifted from being to writing, and authority defined as a kind of "unholy scripture," "a scripture that is in exile, wandering about, estranged from its own meaning, a scripture that testamentarily documents the absence of the holy."[38] Derrida's attempt to distinguish himself from Heidegger failed. He tried to do so "by what looked like a scientific claim; but then with his new science he only placed himself above the deplored incompetency of the sciences in general and linguistics in particular."[39] But, in this reading, "Derrida

---

[33] Jürgen Habermas, *The Philosophical Discourse of Modernity*, p. 181.
[34] Ibid.
[35] Ibid. (Emphasis mine.)
[36] Ibid.
[37] Ibid.
[38] Ibid.
[39] Ibid.

develops the history of Being — which is encoded in writing — in another variation from Heidegger." And finally, having made that association, the moral consequences follow: "*He, too, degrades politics and contemporary history to the status of the ontic and the foreground, so as to romp all the more freely, and with a greater wealth of associations, in the sphere of the ontological and the archewriting.*"[40]

If the text ended there, one might be led to draw the same conclusions as one does from the reading of Heidegger. In the end, Derrida is somehow spared the fate of the reading of Heidegger. "Derrida means to go beyond Heidegger; fortunately, he goes back behind him."[41] The *Urtext* which lingers in the background of Derrida's thought is Jewish mysticism. "Derrida returns to the historical locale where mysticism once turned into enlightenment."[42] Hence, he is, in a way, not unlike Adorno, who tried to understand the close relationship between "mysticism" and "enlightenment." In the end, the judgment is that Derrida does not lead us out of the philosophy of the subject. Habermas writes: "It seems to me doubtful that this unique movement of thought could be repeated with the tools of a negative foundationalism; in any case, it could only lead us deeper into the very modernity that Nietzsche and his followers wanted to overcome."[43]

Is this reading fair? Is it true? Fortunately, my task is to try to understand the subject of this book. Those questions will have to be answered, but not here. Let it suffice to suggest the obvious parallels between Habermas and Derrida. Both accept the project of modern philosophy or post-philosophy, namely, to lead us out of the philosophy of the subject. Implicitly or explicitly, both accept Heidegger's definition of the project of modern philosophy. Obviously, this is no cool academic debate. This story reads like the story of Cain and Abel, blood brothers locked in mortal combat for the soul of the European academic tradition. Can the philosophy of the subject really be overcome by a philosophy of language which concentrates on language as argumentation? Here one begins to engage in the most serious confrontation of a position which harbors an uneasy relationship between the unfinished project of modernity and the philosophy of language.

(c) Foucault

Habermas reads Foucault in a more sympathetic way than he reads Derrida. Bataille, not Heidegger, foreshadows the reading of Foucault. What seems to interest Habermas most in his reading of Foucault is the transition from archaeology to genealogy, and the subsequent preoccupation with the theory of power. Habermas poses the question in the following manner: "What,

---

[40] Ibid. (Emphasis mine.)
[41] Ibid., p. 183.
[42] Ibid., p. 184.
[43] Ibid.

then, are the grounds that determine Foucault to shift the meaning of this specific will to knowledge and to truth that is constitutive for the modern form of knowledge in general, and for the human sciences in particular, by *generalizing* this will to knowing self-mastery into a will to power *per se* and to postulate that *all* discourses (by no means only the modern ones) can be shown to have the character of hidden power and derive from the practices of power?"[44] This question isolates a specific assumption, an assumption that "first marks the turning from an archeology of knowledge to a genealogical explanation of the provenance, rise, and fall of those discourse formations that fill the space of history, without gaps and without meaning."[45]

Habermas tries to answer the question. If one takes the question of epistemé, in Heidegger the question of origins, to its logical conclusions, even through the history of Being, one never masters it. "For this reason Foucault will henceforth have to do without the concept of epistemé altogether."[46] Similarly, Foucault gave up on structuralism when he discovered that "structuralism had covertly already supplied the model for the description of the Classical form of knowledge (semiotic representationalism). Thus, overcoming anthropocentric thought by means of structuralism would not have meant a surpassing of Modernity, but only a renewal of the proto-structuralist form of knowledge of the Classical age."[47] Habermas speculates that a further, slightly more complex problem confronted Foucault. If Foucault had stayed with his assumptions about discourse being the link to the network of practices, then he would have had to confront the question of the rules that underlie existing discourses. "Foucault escapes this difficulty when he gives up the autonomy of the forms of knowledge in favor of their foundation within power technologies and *subordinates* the archeology of knowledge to the genealogy that explains the emergence of knowledge from the practices of power."[48]

If these assumptions are correct, Habermas speculates, Foucault can "relinquish the philosophy of the subject without depending on models from structuralism or the history of Being, which, according to his own analysis, are themselves captive to either the Classical or modern form of knowledge."[49] But if this is the case, there is a certain ironic twist. "Foucault only gains this basis by not thinking genealogically when it comes to his *own* genealogical historiography and by rendering unrecognizable the derivation of this transcendental-historicist concept of power."[50]

[44] Ibid., p. 265.
[45] Ibid.
[46] Ibid., pp. 266–7.
[47] Ibid., p. 267.
[48] Ibid., p. 268.
[49] Ibid.
[50] Ibid., p. 269.

At this point, the clue to Habermas's critique begins to emerge. The "*concealed* derivation of the concept of power from the concept of the will to knowledge" is "systematically ambiguous." On the one hand, methodologically, it is like an "historically oriented sociology of knowledge that employs functionalist procedures." On the other, this orientation can be traced back to a "*theory of constitution.*" As with Heidegger and Derrida, Habermas has chosen in his critique of Foucault a standard form of phenomenological critique. Here is said to be found the trace of the philosophy of the subject in Foucault. "Genealogical historiography is supposed to be ... functionalist social science and at the same time historical research into constitutive social science."[51] Thus, states Habermas, Foucault has "taken from the repertoire of the philosophy of the subject."[52] Hence, the conclusion: "Foucault did not think through the aporias of his own approach well enough to see how his theory of power was overtaken by a fate similar to that of the human sciences rooted in the philosophy of the subject."[53]

III   Conclusion

Habermas may be right: to reconstruct philosophy in the shadow of Heidegger may illustrate a certain "moral" weakness. That seems to be the point. Postmodernism, under the guise of Foucault and particularly Derrida, having placed itself under the Heideggerian banner, represents a certain moral vacuity, an absence of the proper place for the normative question. Hence, like Heidegger, postmodernism gives up on moral standards and in so doing stands ready for the simple seduction by any political system that happens to come along. As those before them, these later philosophers are said to have succumbed, in their own peculiar manner, to the dialectic of enlightenment. They too have fallen into the trap of subject-centered reason, the lingering trace of the mysterious transcendental which seems to lurk beneath their work like a subterranean paradigm. As Heidegger named his mentor, Husserl, so Habermas names Foucault and Derrida as those unable to overcome the legacy of our most recent post-Kantian, post-Husserlian philosophical tradition.

Habermas has laid the charge of subject-centered philosophy at the feet of those most contemporary Continental philosophers by both reading it through the tradition closest to him, the tradition beginning with Hegel, and applying it to those who have also drunk freely from the same well-

---

[51] Ibid., p. 274.
[52] Ibid.
[53] Ibid.

spring. However, the charge in question, as suggested earlier, could have been made by Heidegger himself. That Habermas repeats the early Heidegger by naming this as the problem should perhaps come as no surprise in a world that has been shaped, more or less, by the phenomenological movement, as German philosophy was, particularly by Husserl and the peculiarly Husserlian preoccupation with the transcendental ego.

The disagreement with Heidegger, then, is not with the problem that modern philosophy had to face, but with the path that Heidegger chose in order to overcome the modern dilemma. Heidegger moved in two directions which Habermas found unappealing: first by reduplicating Nietzsche's attempt to avoid modernity by returning to the origins of Western culture, and second by imbibing deeply, too deeply, in the context of German thought of the thirties, i.e., the politics of National Socialism. Given this interpretation, both moves left Heidegger with a position that was not only, in its desire to reconstruct a history of Being, presumptuous, but, in its underlying desire to avoid an indulgence in a certain moment in German history, morally vacuous. Given this reading, that which was so brilliantly disguised can be exposed as pure philosophical pretension. It is but a short step to see those who followed Heidegger to be fated in the same manner.

However, against this backdrop, Habermas has chosen a route that is as dangerous as those he so freely criticizes, namely, to rehabilitate a "passion" which later German philosophy, à la Heidegger, sought to put to rest (a passion which would delight Husserl), namely, the rehabilitation of a form of transcendental argument. Our skeptic, whom we conveniently left behind some chapters ago, would want to know precisely how one can assert the primacy of the transcendental and, at the same time, avoid the charge of attempting to rehabilitate subject-centered reason. No doubt Habermas believes that the way to move beyond Heidegger is to go behind him. Whether or not this is a worthy retrospective path to follow, it seems there is something here which might at least titillate the suspicious mind. Is this really the way to avoid subject-centered philosophy? The preference for a kind of argument which places logic over rhetoric, the rationalistic over the metaphorical, could be read by some as the very attempt to resurrect the kind of subject-centered philosophy of which Husserl was the example *par excellence*.[54] Of course, by now we are familiar with Habermas's arguments: the reconstruction of a philosophy of language as a theory of rationality, based on the logic of speech acts which places the illocutionary as originary and then goes on to see, in the originary force of an utterance, the logical

---

[54] One of the weakest, but at the same time most revealing, sections of *The Philosophical Discourse of Modernity* is the one entitled "On leveling the genre distinction between philosophy and literature" where Habermas mounts a strong defence of the logical over and against Derrida's critique of it. Ibid., pp. 185–210.

intersubjective primacy of speech over consciousness through a kind of argument which searches for the conditions for the possibility contained in every speech act, is supposed to reconstitute the transcendental in a linguistic sphere. But certainly this kind of philosophizing owes as much to *Bewustseinsphilosophie* as it does to *Sprachphilosophie.*

Clearly, I have no desire to defend Heidegger here. Habermas's critique as moral critique may stand. However, a cursory look at what has come to be called the phenomenological movement finds that the critique of what Habermas calls subject-centered philosophy was made, not merely by Heidegger, but also by the second and third generation of the phenomenological movement. One might add parenthetically that analytic thought, following the later Wittgenstein, follows a similar direction. Against this background, what appears questionable in the Habermasian critique of Heidegger, and hence in his critique of postmodernism, is the assumption that to partake in the Heideggerian enterprise leads somehow to a certain "moral vacuity." Indeed, that the particular direction taken by the later Heidegger leads to a "cover up" of his more active political participation in National Socialism need not be doubted. However, it need not follow from this critique that the way out of this dilemma is the resurrection of a certain form of transcendental argumentation that is essentially pre-Heideggerian. Consequently, the guilt by association argument, made against various forms of postmodern philosophy, need not necessarily follow as the logical consequence of the Heideggerian *Kehre.*

The argument against Heidegger is one for a particular reading of a modern philosophical tradition that begins with Kant. Habermas wants to develop a certain logic of argumentation reconstructed from aspects of Kant's first two critiques, within an Hegelian framework which emphasizes a certain kind of rational mediation between the scientific, moral, and aesthetic spheres. This "cognitive" reading of the modern philosophical tradition, with its attempt to incorporate aspects both of linguistic philosophy, particularly Austin's and the later Wittgenstein's, and pragmatism, particularly Mead's and Peirce's, does not occur without risk. If the subject of the discourse on modernity is the attempt to overcome subject-centered reason, it does not necessarily follow that those very attempts which are its most venerable representations need be resurrected in the process. Be that as it may. The problem is heightened when the critique focuses on those forms of philosophical thought which defy or have attempted to overcome forms of philosophy in question. Must they submit to the logic of argumentation arguments which they attempted to repudiate? My suspicion is not only that the paradigm Habermas seeks in the tradition begins to fall apart with Nietzsche, but that its immanent dissolution could already be found in Kant's third critique where the kind of rationality appropriate to the aesthetic form cannot be so neatly integrated with the spheres of morality and science.[55] And if that is the case, it does not follow necessarily that all philosophical questions are reducible to questions of the logic of argumentation which can be neatly differentiated into the spheres of science, morality, and aesthetics. It does not follow that the "enlightenment project," which is after all a metaphor, can be redeemed by logic.[56]

My suspicion is that Habermas wants to present us with a reading of the philosophical tradition which fits into a slightly broader argument, an argument refracted though the prism of democratic theory. To be sure, this argument has its own peculiar Germanic twist. The wager is this: democratic theory can be read into modern philosophy in such a manner that it can be linked with the unfinished project of modernity. Hence, in a peculiar way we are driven back to Hegel, not enthusiastically, because he aborted the normative possibility of modernity by reaching behind modernity to a form of argument that breaks with modernity's canon. Hegel's argument failed to generate itself out of itself. However, in a peculiar way, Hegel sets up the argument by providing a model which can be adapted to the democratic reading. Hegel, in other words, almost provides us with a communicative reading of the philosophical tradition. To stick with the Hegelian reading is to sustain a tacit agreement with the model Hegel establishes. There is a not too subtle message here. To depart from the Hegelian paradigm will mean to depart from the emerging potential of communicative thought. Of course, there is always the question of how to interpret the paradigm. The Hegelians of the left and the right, in both their nineteenth and twentieth century forms, offer examples of false alternatives. Yet, given the combination of the paradigm and a predilection for democratic theory, the path of Nietzsche, Heidegger and postmodernity is relatively easy to chart. By opting out of this tradition, they can be understood to have given up on the normative question. Hence, postmodernism can be appropriately dismissed.

But there is a sub-text here. Behind the Hegelian paradigm lies Kant, the Kant of the first and particularly the second critiques. In this view, the problem of democracy is definitely not a problem of communities or of history; the problem of democracy is essentially one of justification to be explicated by the logic of argumentation. Perhaps the reason for this move

---

[55] This brings us back to the dilemma raised in the first chapter. Because Habermas embarks on a particular reading of modernity which focuses on a unified theory of rationality, derived more or less from Hegel, he reduces the aesthetic which, after Kant's *Critique of Judgment*, cannot be reduced to a mere alternative form of rationality. As such his analysis will serve to undermine the very aesthetic elements upon which his own project rests.

[56] The terms "enlightenment project" and the "communication thesis" are metaphors whose legitimacy remains outside the realm of logic.

lies neither in the texts of Kant nor of Hegel, but in those of Marx. The task has been to reconstruct the unfinished project of modernity by this wedding of the best of Marxism and democratic theory in such a manner that the problem of democracy, as the problem of language, as the problem of morality, as the problem of law, becomes a problem of justification. Whether or not this movement from the traditions establishing democracy to the realm of the transcendental, correlated, to be sure, with the empirical, is necessary (one could divide the philosophical community on this issue), remains the subject of future discussion.

Jürgen Habermas: A Bibliography

René Görtzen
Free University, Amsterdam
For: Mrs U. Habermas-Wesselhoeft

Contents

I Primary Literature

(a) Books by Habermas
(b) Translations into English.
(c) Tanslations into French

II Secondary Literature

(a) Books on Habermas
(b) Communicative Action, Theory of
(c) Consensus Theory of Truth
(d) Education/Pedagogics
(e) Ethics/Moral Development
(f) Hermeneutics/Gadamer
(g) 'Historikerstreit'
(h) Knowledge and Human Interests
(i) Legitimation Crisis
(j) Marx/Marxism
(k) Marxistic Critique, Orthodox—
(l) Modernism—Postmodernism
(m) Positivist Dispute/Social Science
(n) Psychoanalysis/Freud
(o) Public Sphere
(p) Student Protest
(q) Theology/Religion
(r) Work and Interaction

For a complete biliography of primary literature and also more than 900 publications on Habermas, see my *Jürgen Habermas: Eine Bibliographie seiner Schriften und der Sekundärliteratur 1952–1981*. Frankfurt am Main: Suhrkamp 1982. A revised, up-dated version with more than 3000 publications on Habermas will be published at the end of 1990.

I Primary Literature

I (a) *Books by Habermas*

1954 *Das Absolute und die Geschichte. Von der Zwiespältigkeit in Schellings Denken.* Inaugural–Dissertation Philosophie. Bonn, 424 p.

1961 *Student und Politik. Eine soziologische Untersuchung zum politischen Bewusstsein Frankfurter Studenten.* Co-authors: Ludwig von Friedeburg, Christoph Oehler, Friedrich Weltz. Neuwied/Berlin: Luchterhand, 359 p.

1962 *Strukturwandel der Öffentlichkeit. Untersuchungen zu einer Kategorie der bürgerlichen Gesellschaft.* Neuwied/Berlin: Luchterhand, 291 p.

1963 *Theorie und Praxis. Sozialphilosophische Studien.* Neuwied/Berlin: Luchterhand, 379 p. (c.f. 1971).

1967 'Zur Logik der Sozialwissenschaften', in: *Philosophische Rundschau* 14, Beiheft 5, 195 p. (c.f. 1970)

1968 *Erkenntnis und Interesse.* Frankfurt am Main: Suhrkamp, 364 p.

1968 *Technik und Wissenschaft als "Ideologie."* Frankfurt am Main: Suhrkamp, 167 p.

1969 *Protestbewegung und Hochschulreform.* Frankfurt am Main: Suhrkamp, 275 p.

1970 *Zur Logik der Sozialwissenschaften.* Frankfurt am Main: Suhrkamp, 329 p. (Expanded edition from 1967; see also 1982).

1970 *Arbeit–Erkenntnis–Fortschritt. Aufsätze 1954–1979.* Amsterdam: de Munter, 470 p. (=Pirate edition).

1971 *Philosophisch–politische Profile.* Frankfurt am Main: Suhrkamp, 254 p. (c.f. 1981).

1971 *Theorie der Gesellschaft oder Sozialtechnologie. Was leistet die Systemforschung.* Co-author: Niklas Luhmann. Frankfurt am Main: Suhrkamp, 405 p.

1971 *Theorie und Praxis.* Frankfurt am Main: Suhrkamp, 466 p. (Fourth edition, revised, expanded and with a new introduction; cf. 1963).

1973 *Arbeit–Freizeit–Konsum. Frühe Aufsätze.* 's Gravenhage: Eversdijck, 80 p. (= Pirate edition).

1973 *Kultur und Kritik. Verstreute Aufsätze.* Frankfurt am Main: Suhrkamp, 401 p.

1973 *Legitimationsprobleme im Spätkapitalismus.* Frankfurt am Main: Suhrkamp, 196 p.

1974 *Zwei Reden. Aus Anlass der Verleihung des Hegel–Preises 1973 der Stadt Stuttgart an Jürgen Habermas am 19. Januar 1974.* Co-author: Dieter Henrich. Frankfurt am Main: Suhrkamp, 84 p.

1976 *Zur Rekonstruktion des Historischen Materialismus.* Frankfurt am Main: Suhrkamp, 346 p.

1978 *Politik, Kunst, Religion. Essays über zeitgenössische Philosophen.* Stuttgart: Reclam, 151 p.

1979 *Das Erbe Hegels. Zwei Reden aus Anlass der Verleihung des Hegel–Preises 1979 der Stadt Stuttgart an Hans-Georg Gadamer am 13. Juni 1979.* Co-author: Hans-Georg Gadamer. Frankfurt am Main, 94 p.

1981 *Kleine Politische Schriften (I–IV).* Frankfurt am Main: Suhrkamp, 535 p.

1981 *Philosophische-politische Profile.* Frankfurt am Main: Suhrkamp, 479 p. (Third, expanded edition; cf. 1971)

1981 *Theorie des kommunikativen Handelns*. Band 1: *Handlungsrationalität und gesellschaftliche Rationalisierung*. Band 2: *Zur Kritik der funktionalistische Vernunft*. Frankfurt am Main: Suhrkamp, 1167 p.

1982 *Zur Logik der Sozialwissenschaften*. Frankfurt am Main: Suhrkamp, 607 p. (Fifth, expanded edition; cf. 1970)

1983 *Moralbewusstsein und kommunikatives Handeln*. Frankfurt am Main: Suhrkamp, 208 p.

1984 *Vorstudien und Ergänzungen zur Theorie des kommunikativen Handelns*. Frankfurt am Main: Suhrkamp, 607 p.

1985 *Die Neue Unübersichtlichkeit. Kleine Politische Schriften V*. Frankfurt am Main: Suhrkamp, 269 p.

1985 *Der philosophische Diskurs der Moderne*. Zwölf Vorlesungen. Frankfurt am Main: Suhrkamp, 450 p.

1987 *Eine Art Schadensabwicklung. Kleine Politische Schriften VI*. Frankfurt am Main: Suhrkamp, 180 p.

1988 *Nachmetaphysisches Denken. Philosophische Aufsätze*. Frankfurt am Main: Suhrkamp, 286 p.

I (b) Translated into English

1971 *Knowlegde and Human Interests*. Boston: Beacon Press and London: Heinemann, 356 p.

1971 *Toward a Rational Society. Student Protest, Science and Politics*. London: Heinemann, 132 p.

1974 *Theory and Practice*. London: Heinemann, 310 p.

1975 *Legitimation Crisis*. Boston: Beacon Press 1975 and London: Heinemann 1976, 176 p.

1979 *Communication and the Evolution of Society*. Boston: Beacon Press, 239 p.

1983 *Philosophical—Political Profiles*. London: Heinemann, 211 p.

1984 *Theory of Communicative Action*. vol. 1: *Reason and the Rationalization of Society*. Boston: Beacon Press and Cambridge: Polity Press in association with Basil Blackwell, Oxford, 465 p.

1986 *Autonomy and Solidarity. Interviews*. Ed. and introduced by Peter Dews. London: Verso, 219 p.

1987 *The Philosophical Discourse of Modernity. Twelve Lectures*. Cambridge, MA: MIT Press, 430 p.

1987 *The Theory of Communicative Action*. vol. 2: *Lifeworld and System: A Critique of Functionalist Reason*. Boston: Beacon Press and Cambridge: Polity Press in association with Basil Blackwell, Oxford, 457 p.

1988 *On the Logic of the Social Sciences*. Cambridge, MA: MIT Press and Cambridge: Polity Press in association with Basil Blackwell, Oxford, 220 p.

1989 *Moral Consciousness and Communicative Action*. Cambridge, MA: MIT Press, c. 220 p.

1989 *The Structural Transformation of the Public Sphere*. Cambridge, MA: MIT Press, c. 300 p.

I (c)   *Translated into French*

1973   *La Technique et la science comme 'idéologie.'* Paris: Gallimard, 211 p.
1974   *Profils philosophiques et politiques.* Paris: Gallimard, 293 p.
1975   *Théorie et pratique.* Paris: Payot, vol. 1, 240 p.; vol. 2, 238 p.
1976   *Connaissance et Intérêt.* Paris: Gallimard, 386 p.
1978   *L'Espace public. Archéologie de la publicité comme dimension constitutive de la société bourgeoise.* Paris: Payot, 328 p.
1978   *Raison et légitimité. Problèmes de légitimation dans le capitalisme avancé.* Paris: Payot, 212 p.
1985   *Après Marx.* Paris: Fayard, 341 p. (= *Zur Rekonstruktion des Historischen Materialismus* 1976).
1987   *Logique des sciences sociales et autres essais.* Paris: Presses Universitaires de France, 459 p.
1987   *Morale et communication. Conscience morale et activité communicationnelle.* Paris: Les Editions du Cerf, 213 p.
1987   *Théorie de l'agir communicationnel.* 1. *Rationalité de l'agir et rationalisation de la société.* 2. *Pour une critique de la raison fonctionnaliste.* Paris: Fayard, vol. 1: 448 p., vol. 2: 480 p.
1988   *Le discours philosophique de la modernité. Douze conférences.* Paris: Gallimard, 485 p.
1988   *Martin Heidgger. L'oeuvre et l'engagement.* Paris: Les Editions du Cerf, 73 p.

II   Secondary Literature

II (a)   Books on Habermas

Alford, C. Fred: *Science and the Revenge of Nature: Marcuse & Habermas.* Tampa, FLA: University of South Florida Press and Gainesville, FLA: University of Florida Press 1985, 226 p.

Arens, Edmund (ed.), *Habermas und die Theologie. Beiträge zur theologischen Rezeption, Diskussion und Kritik der Theorie kommunikativen Handelns.* Düsseldorf: Patmos Verlag 1989, 270 p.

Assoun, Paul-Laurent and Gérard Raulet: *Marxisme et théorie critique.* Paris: Payot 1978, 248 p.

Bahr, Hans-Dieter: *Kritik der 'Politischen Technologie'. Eine Auseinandersetzung mit Herbert Marcuse und Jürgen Habermas.* Frankfurt am Main: Europäische Verlagsanstalt 1970, 107 p.

Bauer, Karl: *Der Denkweg von Jürgen Habermas zur Theorie des kommunikativen Handelns. Grundlagen einer neuen Fundamentaltheologie?* Regensburg: S. Roderer Verlag 1987, 455 p.

Bernstein, Richard J.: *Habermas and Modernity.* Cambridge: Polity Press and Oxford: Basil Blackwell 1985, 243 p.

Bilden, Helga: *Das unhistorische Subjekt. Zur Kritik sozialisationstheoretischer Grundkonzepte.* Weinheim, Basel: Beltz 1977, 278 p.

Brand, Arie: *The Force of Reason. An Introduction to the Work of Jürgen Habermas.* Sydney and London: Allen & Unwin 1989, 144 p.

Brinkmann, Dörte: *Das Theorie–Praxis–Problem bei Marx und Habermas.* Hamburg: Presseverlag Knut Reim 1976, 247 p.

Brüggemann, Beate: *Die Utopie der besseren Verständigung. Zur Rekonstruktion des Identitätskonzeptes.* Frankfurt am Main and New York: Campus 1980, 171 p.

Bühner, Bernd and Achim Birnmeyer: *Ideologie und Diskurs. Zur Theorie von Jürgen Habermas und ihrer Rezeption in der Pädagogik.* Frankfurt am Main: Haag + Herchen 1982, 317 p.

Dallmayr, Winfried (ed.): *Materialien zu Habermas' "Erkenntnis und Interesse".* Frankfurt am Main: Suhrkamp 1974, 434 p.

Danielzyk, Rainer and Fritz Rüdiger (eds). *Vernunft der Moderne? Zu Habermas' "Theorie des kommunikativen Handelns".* Münster: edition liberación 1986, 157 p.

DeHaven-Smit, Lance: *Philosophical Critiques of Policy Analysis: Lindblom, Habermas, and the Great Society.* Gainesville, FLA: University of Florida Press 1988, 156 p.

Ealy, Steven D.: *Communication, Speech and Politics: Habermas and Political Analysis.* Washington, DC: University Press of America 1981, 245 p.

Ferry, Jean-Marc: *Habermas, l'éthique de la communication.* Paris: Presses Universitaires de France 1987, 587 p.

Feuerstein, Thomas: *Emanzipation und Rationalität einer kritischen Erziehungswissenschaft. Methodologische Grundlagen im Anschluß an Habermas.* München: Kösel 1973, 143 p.

Forester, John (ed.), *Critical Theory and Public Life.* Cambridge, MA and London: MIT Press 1985, 337 p.

Frank, Manfred: *Die Grenzen der Verständigung. Ein Geistergespräch zwischen Lyotard und Habermas.* Frankfurt am Main: Suhrkamp 1988, 103 p.

Gamm, Gerhard: *Eindimensionale Kommunikation. Vernunft und Rhetorik in Jürgen Habermas' "Deutung der Moderne."* Würzburg: Königshausen + Neumann 1987, 84 p.

Geiss, Imanuel: *Die Habermas-Kontroverse. Ein deutscher Streit.* Berlin: Siedler Verlag 1988, 207 p.

Geuss, Raymond: *The Idea of a Critical Theory. Habermas and the Frankfurt School.* Cambridge: Cambridge University Press 1981, 100 p. German: *Die Idee einer Kritischen Theorie.* Königstein/Ts.: Hain 1983, 117 p.

Giegel, Hans-Joachim: *System und Krise. Kritik der Luhmannschen Gesellschaftstheorie. Beitrag zur Habermas-Luhmann-Diskussion.* Supplement III. Frankfurt am Main: Suhrkamp 1975, 193 p.

Glaser, Wilhelm R.: *Soziales und instrumentales Handeln. Probleme der Technologie bei Arnold Gehlen und Jürgen Habermas.* Stuttgart: W. Kohlhammer 1972, 216 p.

Görtzen, René: *Jürgen Habermas: Eine Bibliographie seiner Schriften und der Sekundärliteratur 1952–1981.* Frankfurt am Main: Suhrkamp 1982, 230 p.

Gripp, Helga: *Jürgen Habermas. Und es gibt sie doch–Zur kommunikationstheoretischen Begründung von Vernunft bei Jürgen Habermas.* Paderborn: F. Schöningh 1984, 153 p.

Habermas, Jürgen. *L'activité communicationelle.* Textes de C. Bouchindhomme, J.-M. Ferry, J. Habermas, R. Rochlitz. Lille: Université de Lille III 1987, 100 p. [= *Les Cahiers de Philosophie,* no. 3]

Heidorn, Joachim: *Legitimität und Regierbarkeit. Studien zu den Legitimitätstheorien von Max Weber, Niklas Luhmann, Jürgen Habermas und der Unregierbarkeitsforschung.* Berlin: Duncker & Humblot 1982, 295 p.

Held, David: *Introduction to Critical Theory. Horkheimer to Habermas.* London: Hutchinson 1980, 511 p.

Höhn, Hans-Joachim: *Kirche und kommunikatives Handeln. Studien zur Theologie und Praxis der Kirche in der Auseinandersetzung mit den Sozialtheorien Niklas Luhmann und Jürgen Habermas.* Frankfurt am Main: Josef Knecht 1985, 298 p.

Holzer, Horst: *Kommunikation oder gesellschaftliche Arbeit. Zur Theorie des kommunikativen Handelns von Jürgen Habermas.* Berlin-Ost: Akademie-Verlag 1987, 130 p.

Honneth, Axel: *Kritik der Macht. Reflexionsstufen einer kritischen Gesellschaftstheorie.* Frankfurt am Main: Suhrkamp 1985, 382 p.

—— and Hans Joas (eds): *Kommunikatives Handeln. Beiträge zu Jürgen Habermas' "Theorie des kommunikativen Handelns."* Frankfurt am Main: Suhrkamp 1986, 420 p.

—— Thomas McCarthy, Claus Offe and Albrecht Wellmer (eds), *Zwischenbetrachtungen. Im Prozeß der Aufklärung. Jürgen Habermas zum 60. Geburtstag.* Frankfurt am Main: Suhrkamp 1989, 839 p.

Horster, Detlef: *Habermas zur Einführung.* Hannover: SOAK 1980, 124 p. Revised and expanded edition in 1988, 157 p.

Ingram, David: *Habermas and the Dialectic of Reason.* New Haven, CT and London: Yale University Press 1987, 263 p.

Jäger, Wolfgang: *Öffentlichkeit und Parlamentarismus. Eine Kritik an Jürgen Habermas.* Stuttgart: W. Kohlhammer 1973, 107 p.

Jakob, Samuel: *Zwischen Gespräch und Diskurs. Untersuchungen zur sozialhermeneutischen Begründung der Agogik anhand einer Gegenüberstellung von Hans-Georg Gadamer und Jürgen Habermas.* Bern, Stuttgart: Paul Haupt 1985, 312 p.

Kaiser, Hans-Rainer: *Staat und gesellschaftliche Integration. Zur Analyse und Kritik des Staatsbegriffs bei Jürgen Habermas und Claus Offe.* Marburg: Verlag Arbeiterbewegung und Gesellschaftswissenschaft 1977, 123 p.

Keat, Russell: *The Politics of Social Theory. Habermas, Freud and the Critique of Positivism.* Chicago: University of Chicago Press and Oxford: Basil Blackwell 1981, 245 p.

Kessler, Alfred: *Identität und Kritik. Zu Habermas' Interpretation des psychoanalytischen Prozesses.* Würzburg: Königshausen + Neumann 1983, 97 p.

Kimmerle, Gerd: *Verwerfungen. Vergleichende Studien zu Adorno und Habermas.* Tübingen: edition diskord im Konkursbuchverlag 1986, 219 p.

Kiss, Gábor: *Paradigmawechsel in der Kritischen Theorie: Jürgen Habermas' intersubjektiver Ansatz.* Stuttgart: Enke 1987, 122 p.

Koch, friedhelm: *Jürgen Habermas' "Theorie des kommunikativen Handelns" als Kritik von Geschichtsphilosophie.* Frankfurt am Main, Bern and New York: Peter Lang 1985, 272 p.

Koreng, Christine: *Norm und Interaktion bei Jürgen Habermas.* Düsseldorf: Patmos 1979, 136 p.

Kortian, Garbis: *Métacritique.* Paris: Les Editions de Minuit 1979, 132 p. *English:*

Metacritique. The Philosophical Argument of Jürgen Habermas. Cambridge: Cambridge University Press 1980, 135 p.

Kritik und Interpretation der Kritischen Theorie. Aufsätze über Adorno, Horkheimer, Marcuse, Benjamin, Habermas. Giessen: A. Achenbach 1970, 383 p.

Kunstmann, Wilfried: *Gesellschaft — Emanzipation — Diskurs. Darstellung und Kritik der Gesellschaftstheorie von Jürgen Habermas.* München: W. Fink 1977, 128 p.

Lauenstein, Diether: *Das Ich und die Gesellschaft. Einführung in die philosophische Soziologie im Kontrast zu Max Weber und Jürgen Habermas in der Denkweise Plotins und Fichtes.* Stuttgart: Verlag Freies Geistesleben 1974, 367 p.

Ley, Hermann and Thomas Müller: *Kritische Vernunft und Revolution. Zur Kontroverse zwischen Hans Albert und Jürgen Habermas.* Köln: Pahl—Rugenstein 1971, 267 p.

Lieth, Winfried: *Martin Buber und Jürgen Habermas. Krise, Dialog und Kommunikation.* Konstanz: Hartung—Gorre 1988, 209 p.

Linkenbach, Antje: *Opake Gestalten des Denkens. Jürgen Habermas und die Rationalität fremder Lebensformen.* München: Wilhelm Fink 1986, 313 p.

McCarthy, Thomas A.: *The Critical Theory of Jürgen Habermas.* Cambridge, MA and London: MIT Press 1978, 466 p. German: *Kritik der Verständigungsverhältnisse. Zur Theorie von Jürgen Habermas.* Frankfurt am Main: Suhrkamp 1980, 551 p.

Maciejewski, Franz (ed.): *Theorie der Gesellschaft oder Sozialtechnologie. Beiträge zur Habermas—Luhmann—Diskussion.* Supplement I. Frankfurt am Main: Suhrkamp 1973, 211 p.

—— (ed.): *Theorie der Gesellschaft oder Sozialtechnologie. Neue Beiträge zur Habermas—Luhmann—Diskussion.* Supplement II. Frankfurt am Main: Suhrkamp 1974, 236 p.

Maier, M. Frumentia: *Entwicklungslogik und Reziprozität Kommunikativer Ethik. Eine inhaltsanalytische Untersuchung zum Einfluß Kritischer Theorie (Habermas) auf die Gestaltung von Curricula im Elementarbereich — unter besonderer Berücksichtigung des Begründungszusammenhangs Piaget—Habermas.* Frankfurt am Main: Haag + Herchen 1980, 644 p.

Matthiesen, Ulf: *Das Dickicht der Lebenswelt und die Theorie des kommunikativen Handelns.* München: W. Fink (1983/84), 186 p.

Maurer, Reinhart Klemens: *Jürgen Habermas' Aufhebung der Philosophie.* Philosophische Rundschau 1977, Beiheft 8, 70 p.

Meyer, Thomas: *Zwischen Spekulation und Erfahrung. Einige Bemerkungen zur Wissenschaftstheorie von Jürgen Habermas.* Frankfurt am Main: Makol 1972, 72 p.

Nacke, Bernhard: *Normenbegründung und politische Praxis. Orientierungshilfe durch herrschaftsfreien Diskurs bei Jürgen Habermas und philosophischen Diskurs bei Willi Oelmüller?* Essen: Die Blaue Eule 1986, 140 p.

Nagl, Ludwig: *Gesellschaft und Autonomie. Historisch—systematische Studien zur Entwicklung der Sozialtheorie von Hegel bis Habermas.* Wien: Verlag der Österreichische Akademie der Wissenschaften 1983, 351 p.

Negt, Oskar (ed.): *Die Linke antwortet Jürgen Habermas.* Frankfurt am Main: Europäische Verlagsanstalt 1968, 211 p.

New German Critique, no. 35, 1985, spring—summer: "Special Issue on Jürgen Habermas," 186 p.

Pojana, Manfred: *Zum Konzept der kommunikativen Rationalität bei Jürgen Habermas.* Essen: Die Blaue Eule 1985, 132 p.

Pusey, Michael: *Jürgen Habermas.* Chichester: Ellis Horwood and London and New York: Tavistock 1987, 128 p.

Reijen, Willem van and Karl–Otto Apel (eds): *Rationales Handeln und Gesellschaftstheorie.* Bochum: Germinal Verlag 1984, 240 p.

Rendtorff, Trutz: *Gesellschaft ohne Religion? Theologische Aspekte einer sozialtheoretischen Kontroverse (Luhmann–Habermas).* München: Piper 1975, 101 p.

Rockmore, Tom: *Habermas on Historical Materialism.* Bloomington, IL and Indianapolis: Indiana University Press 1989, 202 p.

Roderick, Rick: *Habermas and the Foundations of Critical Theory.* Basingstoke and London: Macmillan 1986, 194 p.

Rüddenklau, Eberhard: *Gesellschaftliche Arbeit oder Arbeit und Interaktion? Zum Stellenwert des Arbeitsbegriffes bei Habermas, Marx und Hegel.* Frankfurt am Main, Bern: Peter Lang 1982, 422 p.

Schrape, Klaus: *Theorien normativer Strukturen und ihres Wandels.* Teil I: *Theoretische Einführung, Rekonstruktion und Kritik der Theorie von Jürgen Habermas.* Basel: Social Strategies Publishers Co-operative Society 1977, 261 p.

Sensat Jr, Julius: *Habermas and Marxism. An Appraisal.* Beverly Hills and London: Sage 1979, 176 p.

Siebert, Rudolf J.: *From Critical Theory of Society to Theology of Communicative Praxis.* Washington, DC: University Press of America 1979, 223 p.

—— *The Critical Theory of Religion. The Frankfurt School. From Universal Pragmatic to Political Theology.* Berlin, New York, and Amsterdam: Mouton 1985, 722 p.

Simon-Schäfer, Roland and Walther Ch. Zimmerli: *Theorie zwischen Kritik und Praxis. Jürgen Habermas und die Frankfurter Schule.* Stuttgart/Bad Cannstatt: Frommann–Holzboog 1975, 186 p.

Theunissen, Michael: *Kritische Theorie der Gesellschaft. Zwei Studien.* Berlin and New York: W. de Gruyter 1981, 57 p.

Thompson, John B.: *Critical Hermeneutics. A Study in the Thought of Paul Ricoeur and Jürgen Habermas.* Cambridge and London: Cambridge University Press 1981, 257 p.

—— and David Held (eds): *Habermas. Critical Debates.* London and Basingstoke: Macmillan 1982, 324 p.

Tuschling, Burkhard: *Die "offene" und die "abstrakte" Gesellschaft. Habermas und die Konzeption von Vergesellschaftung der klassisch-bürgerlichen Rechts- und Staatsphilosophie.* Berlin: Argument-Verlag 1978, 492 p.

Weihe, Ulrich: *Diskurs und Komplexität. Eine Auseinandersetzung mit dem Handlungsbezug der Gesellschaftslehren von Habermas und Luhmann.* Stuttgart: Hochschulverlag 1979, 211 p.

Wellmer, Albrecht: *Kritische Gesellschaftstheorie und Positivismus.* Frankfurt am Main: Suhrkamp 1969, 148 p. English: *Critical Theory of Society.* New York: Herder and Herder 1971, 139 p.

—— *Ethik und Dialog. Elemente des moralischen Urteils bei Kant und in der Diskursethik.* Frankfurt am Main: Suhrkamp 1986, 224 p.

White, Stephen: *The recent work of Jürgen Habermas. Reason, justice and modernity.* Cambridge: Cambridge University Press 1988, 190 p.

Willms, Bernard: *Kritik und Politik. Jürgen Habermas oder das politische Defizit der "Kritischen Theorie"*. Frankfurt am Main: Suhrkamp 1973, 207 p.

Zimmermann, Rolf: *Utopie — Rationalität — Politik. Zu Kritik, Rekonstruktion und Systematik einer emanzipatorischen Gesellschaftstheorie bei Marx und Habermas.* Freiburg, München: Karl Alber 1985, 461 p.

Die Zukunft der Vernunft. Eine Auseinandersetzung. Participants: Wolfgang Bonß, Helmut Dubiel e.o. Tübingen: edition diskord im Konkursbuchverlag 1985, 149 p.

II (b)   Communicative Action Theory of *

Alexander, Jeffrey C.: 'Review Essay: Habermas' New Critical Theory: Its Promise and Problems', in: *American Journal of Sociology*, vol. 91, 1985, no. 2, pp. 400–24.

Baxter, Hugh: 'System and Life-World in Habermas's Theory of Communicative Action', in: *Theory and Society*, vol. 16, 1987, no. 1, pp. 39–86.

Berger, Johannes: 'Die Versprachlichung des Sakralen und die Entsprachlichung der Ökonomie', in: *Zeitschrift für Soziologie*, vol. 11, 1982, no. 4, pp. 353–65.

Bogen, David E.: 'A reappraisal of Habermas's Theory of Communicative Action in the light of detailed investigations of social praxis', in: *Journal for the Theory of Social Behavior*, vol. 19, 1989, no. 1 (March), pp. 47–77.

Bohman, James F.: 'Formal Pragmatics and Social Criticism: The Philosophy of Language and the Critique of Ideology in Habermas's Theory of Communicative Action', in: *Philosophy & Social Criticism*, vol. 11, 1986, no. 4, pp. 331–53.

Breuer, Stefan: 'Die Depotenzierung der Kritischen Theorie. Über Jürgen Habermas' "Theory des kommunikativen Handelns"', in: *Leviathan*, vol. 10, 1982, no. 1, pp. 132–46.

Brunkhorst, Hauke: 'Kommunikative Vernunft und rächende Gewalt', in: *Sozialwissenschaftliche Literatur Rundschau*, vol. 6, 1983, no. 8–9, pp. 7–34.

Bubner, Rüdiger: 'Rationalität als Lebensform. Zu Jürgen Habermas' "Theorie des kommunikativen Handelns"', in: *Merkur*, vol. 36, 1982, no. 4, pp. 341–55.

Christoph, Klaus: 'Am Anfang war das Wort. Zur Gesellschaftstheorie von Jürgen Habermas' in: *Leviathan. Zeitschrift für Sozialwissenschaft* (Berlin), vol. 13, 1985, no. 4, pp. 334–56.

Collins, Randall: 'Habermas and the Search for Reason', in: *Semiotica* (Amsterdam), vol. 64, 1987, no. 1–2, pp. 157–69.

Dallmayr, Fred R.: 'Life-World and Communicative Action', in: ibid., *Polis and Praxis. Exercises in Contemporary Political Theory.* Cambridge, MA: MIT Press 1984, pp. 224–53. (Here also on Habermas: 'Is Critical Theory a Humanism?', pp. 133–65).

Deroche, Lilyane: 'Morale et communication', in: *L'année sociologique* (Paris), vol. 38, 1988, pp. 362–73.

* For an expanded survey of literature about Habermas's Theory of Communication Action, see my "Bibliographire zur Theorie des Kommunikativen Handelns", in: A. Honneth, H. Joas (eds), *Kommun: katives Handeln. Beiträge zu Jürgen Habermas' "Theorie des kommunikativen Handelns"*. Frankfurt am Main: Suhrkamp 1986, pp. 406–16.

Dux, Günter: 'Die Rekonstruktion der Anfänge', in: *Soziologische Revue*, vol. 5, 1982, no. 4, pp. 381–9.

Freitag, Barbara: 'Theorie des kommunikativen Handelns und Genetische Psychologie. Ein Dialog zwischen Jürgen Habermas und Jean Piaget', in: *Kölner Zeitschrift für Soziologie und Sozialpsychologie*, vol. 35, 1983, no. 3, pp. 555–76.

Furth, Hans: 'A Developmental Perspective on the Societal Theory of Habermas', in *Human Development*, vol. 26, 1983, no. 4, pp. 181–97.

Giddens, Anthony: 'Reason without Revolution? Habermas' Theorie des kommunikativen Handelns', in *Praxis International*, vol. 2, 1982, no. 3, pp. 318–38.

Groh, Dieter: 'Spuren der Vernunft in der Geschichte. Der Weg von Jürgen Habermas zur "Theorie de kommunikativen Handelns" im Schatten Max Webers', in: *Geschichte und Gesellschaft* (Göttingen), vol. 12, 1986, no. 4, pp. 443–76.

Grondin, Jean: 'Rationalité et agir communicationnel chez Habermas', in: *Critique* (Paris), no. 464–5, 1986, pp. 40–59.

Haarscher, Guy: 'Perelman and Habermas', in: *Law and Philosophy*, vol. 5, 1986, no. 3, pp. 331–42.

Herrlitz, Wolfgang: 'Über Jürgen Habermas' Theorie des kommunikativen Handelns; sprachtheoretischer Hintergrund – sprachdidaktische Perspektiven', in: *Spiegel* (Netherlands), vol. 2, 1984, no. 1, pp. 5–44.

Hesse, Heidrun, 'Widersprüche der Moderne. Einwände gegen Habermas' Konzept kommunikativer Rationalität', in: Gerhard Gamm (ed.), *Angesichts objektiver Verblendung. Über die Paradoxien kritischer Theorie*. Tübingen: edition im Konkursbuchverlag 1985, pp. 252–81.

Honneth, Axel, 'Adorno und Habermas. Zur kommunikationstheoretischen Wende kritischer Sozialphilosophie', in: *Merkur*, vol. 33, 1979, no. 7, pp. 648–65. In English: 'Communication and Reconciliation. Habermas' Critique of Adorno', in: *Telos*, no. 39, 1979, spring, pp. 45–61 (here also a reply of James Schmidt, 'Offensive Critical Theory', pp. 62–70).

Knips, Ignaz: 'Kommunikative Rationalität. Probleme eines diskurstheoretischen Zuganges zur Moderne (Technologiediskussion)', in: *Widerspruch*. Münchner Zeitschrift für Philosophie, vol. 6, 1986, no. 1, pp. 49–60.

—— 'Symbolische Formen und Akteure. Zur Frage einer Individualität des Theoretikers und Autors (P. Bourdieu und J. Habermas)', in: *Widerspruch*. Münchner Zeitschrift für Philosophie, vol. 9, 1989, no. 16–17, pp. 63–75.

Kochinke, Jürgen: 'Versuch, Habermas kritisch zu lesen', in: *Leviathan*. Zeitschrift für Sozialwissenschaft (Berlin), vol. 16, 1988, no. 1, pp. 44–76.

Luhmann, Niklas: 'Autopoiesis, Handlung und kommunikative Verständigung', in: *Zeitschrift für Soziologie*, vol. 11, 1982, no. 4, pp. 366–79.

McCumber, John: 'Philosophy as the Heteronomous Center of Modern Discourse: Jürgen Habermas', in: Hugh J. Silverman (ed.), *Philosophy and Non-Philosophy Since Merleau-Ponty*. London: Routledge and New York: Routledge in association with Routledge, Chapman and Hall 1988, pp. 211–31 and notes, pp. 332–6.

Meschonnic, Henri: 'Le Langage chez Habermas', in: H. Meschonnic (ed.),

Critique de la Théorie Critique. Langage et histoire. Paris: Presses Universitaires de Vincennes 1985, pp. 153−200.

Misgeld, Dieter: 'Communication and societal Rationalization: A Review Essay of Jürgen Habermas' Theorie des kommunikativen Handelns' in: *The Canadian Journal of Sociology*, vol. 8, 1983, no. 4, pp. 433−53.

Münch, Richard: 'Von der Rationalisierung zur Verdinglichung der Lebenswelt?', in: *Soziologische Revue*, vol. 5, 1982, no. 4, pp. 390−7.

Nielsen, Donald A.: 'A Theory of Communicative Action or a Sociology of Civilizations? A Critique of Jürgen Habermas', in: *International Journal of Politics, Culture, and Society*, vol. 1, 1987, no. 1 (fall), pp. 159−88.

Nielsen, Greg Marc: 'Communication et esthétique culturelle dans deux sociologies critiques: J. Habermas et M. Rioux', in: *Sociologie et sociétés* (Montréal), vol. 17, 1985, no. 2, pp. 13−26.

Nolte, Paul: 'Soziologische Theorie und Geschichte. Was können Historiker von Jürgen Habermas' "Theorie des kommunikativen Handelns" lernen?' in: *Geschichte und Gesellschaft* (Göttingen), vol. 12, 1986, no. 4, pp. 530−47.

Nusser, Karl-Heinz: 'Totalität ohne subjekt. Zu Habermas' "Theorie des kommunikativen Handelns"' in: *Zeitschrift für philosophische Forschung*, vol. 39, 1985, no. 4, pp. 590−600.

Pertierra, Raul: 'The Rationality Problematique: An Anthropological Review of Habermas' "Theory of Communicative Action" Volume I', in: *Social Analysis*, no. 23, 1988, August, pp. 72−88.

Rasmussen, David M.: 'Communicative Action and Philosophy: Reflections on Habermas' "Theorie des kommunikativen Handelns", in: *Philosophy & Social Criticism*, vol. 9, 1982, no. 1, pp. 2−28.

Schmidt, James: 'Jürgen Habermas and the Difficulties of Enlightenment', in: *Social Research*, vol. 49, 1982, no. 1, pp. 181−208.

Schnädelbach, Herbert: 'Diskurse', in: ibid., *Reflexion und Diskurs. Fragen einer Logik der Philosophie.* Frankfurt am Main: Suhrkamp 1977, pp. 135−75.

Skjei, Erling: 'A Comment on Performative, Subject, and Proposition in Habermas' "Theory of Communication"', in: *Inquiry*, vol. 28, 1985, no. 1, pp. 87−105 (here also from Habermas: 'Reply to Skjei', pp. 105−13).

Smith, A. Anthony: 'Habermas and History: The Institutionalization of Discourse as Historical Project', in: Bernard P. Dauenhauer (ed.), *At the Nexus of Philosophy and History*. Athens, GA and London: The University of Georgia Press 1987, pp. 201−22.

Spülbeck, Volker: 'Herrschaftsfreie Kommunikation als emanzipatorische Praxis: Jürgen Habermas', in: ibid., *Neomarxismus und Theologie. Gesellschaftskritik in Kritischer Theorie und Politischer Theologie*. Freiburg/Br.: Herder 1977, pp. 109−69.

Tugendhat, Ernst: 'Habermas on Communicative Action', in: Gottfried Seebass and Raimo Tuomela (eds), *Social Action*. Dordrecht, Boston, Lancaster: D. Reidel 1985, pp. 179−86. (Here also articles of Michael Baurmann, pp. 187−96 and Hans Haferkamp, pp. 197−205 on Habermas' *Theory of Communicative Action*.)

Vincent, Jean-Marie: 'Action et communication', in: *L'Année sociologique* (Paris), vol. 34, 1984, pp. 241−53.

Wagner, Gerhard and Heinz Zipprian: 'Macht und Geltung. Bemerkungen zu Jürgen Habermas' sprachtheoretischer Grundlegung der Theorie des kommunikativen Handelns', in: *Leviathan*. Zeitschrift für Sozialwissenschaft, vol. 16, 1988, no. 3, pp. 395−405.

Wellmer, Albrecht: 'Reason, Utopia, and the Dialectic of Enlightenment', in: *Praxis International*, vol. 3, 1983, no. 2, pp. 83−107.

Zimmerli, Walther Ch.: 'Kommunikation und Metaphysik. Zu den Anfangsgründen von Habermas' "Theorie des kommunikativen Handelns"', in: Willi Oelmüller (ed.), *Metaphysik heute?* Paderborn, München: F. Schöningh 1987, pp. 97−111.

II (c) *Consensus Theory of Truth*

Alexy, Robert: 'Habermas' Konsensustheorie der Wahrheit', in: ibid., *Theorie der juristischen Argumentation. Die Theorie des rationalen Diskurses als Theorie der juristischen Begründung.* Frankfurt am Main: Suhrkamp 1978, p. 134−77.

Barley, Delbert: 'Konsensustheorie der Wahrheit bei Jürgen Habermas', in: ibid., *Wissenschaft und Lebenswahrheit. Zwei Bereiche der Wirklichkeitserfahrung.* Stuttgart: Klett-Cotta 1980, p. 105−33.

Beckermann, Ansgar: 'Die realistischen Voraussetzungen der Konsenstheorie von J. Habermas', in: *Zeitschrift für allgemeine Wissenschaftstheorie*, vol. 3, 1972, no. 1, pp. 63−80.

Ferrara, Alessandro: 'A Critique of Habermas's Consensus Theory of Truth', in: *Philosophy & Social Criticism*, vol. 13, 1987, no. 1, pp. 39−67.

Freundlieb, Dieter: 'Zur Problematik einer Diskurstheorie der Wahrheit', in: *Zeitschrift für allgemeine Wissenschaftstheorie*, vol. 6, 1975, no. 1, pp. 82−107.

Gerber, Monika: 'Zur Korrespondenz- und Konsenstheorie der Wahrheit', in: *Zeitschrift für allgemeine Wissenschaftstheorie*, vol. 7, 1976, no. 1, pp. 39−57.

Healy, Paul: 'Is Habermas's Consensus Theory a Theory of Truth?', in: *Irish Philosophical Journal* (Belfast), vol. 4, 1987, pp. 145−52.

Hentig, Hartmut von: 'Konsenstheorie. Über die Schwierigkeit, gemeinsam nützlichen Wahrheiten näherzukommen', in: *Neue Sammlung* (Göttingen), vol. 13, 1973, pp. 265−83.

Hesse, Mary: 'Habermas' Consensus Theory of Truth' in: ibid., *Revolutions and Reconstructions in the Philosophy of Science.* Brighton/Sussex: The Harvester Press 1980, pp. 206−31.

Höffe, Otfried: 'Kritische Überlegungen zur Konsensustheorie der Wahrheit (Habermas)' in: *Philosophisches Jahrbuch* (Freiburg/Br.), vol. 83, 1976, no. 2, pp. 314−332.

Ilting, Karl-Heinz: 'Geltung als Konsens', in: *Neue Hefte für Philosophie* (Göttingen), no. 10, 1976, pp. 20−50.

Keuth, Herbert: 'Erkenntnis oder Entscheidung? Die Konsenstheorien der Wahrheit und der Richtigkeit von Jürgen Habermas', in: *Zeitschrift für allgemeine Wissenschaftstheorie*, vol. 10, 1979, no. 2, pp. 375−93.

Martens, Ekkehard: 'Der Zwang der Wahrheit. Zum Dezisionismusproblem bei Jürgen Habermas', in: *Philosophisches Jahrbuch* (Freiburg/Br.), vol. 83, 1976, no. 2, pp. 392−401.

Scheit, Herbert: *Wahrheit − Diskurs − Demokratie. Studien zur "Konsensus-*

theorie der Wahrheit". Freiburg/München: Karl Alber 1987, 493 p. (Here also: 'Rekonstruktion der "Konsensustheorie der Wahrheit"': Jürgen Habermas', pp. 86–108.)

II (d)   *Education/Pedagogics*

Bärenz, Helmut: 'Diskursbegriff und kritische Erziehungswissenschaft', in: *Pädagogische Rundschau*, vol. 32, 1978, no. 2, pp. 91–111.

Bredo, Eric and Walter Feinberg: 'The Critical Approach to Social and Educational Research', in: ibid. (eds), *Knowledge and Values in Social and Educational Research*. Philadelphia: Temple University Press 1982, pp. 271–91.

Fellsches, Josef: *Moralische Erziehung als politische Bildung*. Heidelberg: Quelle und Meyer 1977, 240 p. On Habermas: 'Kritik der Rollentheorie', pp. 92–8; 'Die Diskurstheorie', pp. 99–107.

Groothoff, Hans-Hermann: 'Zur Bedeutung der Diskursethik von Jürgen Habermas für die Pädagogik', in: *Pädagogische Rundschau*, vol. 39, 1985, no. 3, pp. 275–98.

Lassahn, Rudolf: 'Kritische Erziehungswissenschaft. -Die implizite Bildungstheorie bei J. Habermas', in: ibid., *Einführung in die Pädagogik*. Heidelberg: Quelle und Meyer 1974; 2nd., revised edition in 1976, pp. 125–43.

Mezirow, Jack: 'Concept and Action in Adult Education', in: *Adult Education Quarterly* (Washington), vol. 35, 1985, no. 3, pp. 142–51.

Oelkers, Jürgen: 'Pädagogische Anmerkungen zu Habermas' "Theorie des kommunikativen Handelns"', in: *Zeitschrift für Pädagogik*, vol. 30, 1983, no. 2, pp. 271–80.

Peukert, Helmut: 'Kritische Theorie und Pädagogik', in: *Zeitschrift für Pädagogik*, vol. 30, 1983, no. 2, pp. 195–217.

Reimann, Bruno W.: 'Die Pädagogik des Diskurses in soziologischer Perspektive', in: *Neue Sammlung*, vol. 19, 1979, no. 4, pp. 379–400.

Schäfer, Arnold: *Kritische Kommunikation und gefährdete Identität. Zur anthroposoziologischen Grundlegung einer kritischen Erziehungstheorie*. Stuttgart: Klett-Cotta 1978, 516 p. Especially on Habermas: 'Kooperative Kritik an der Gesellschaft und kritische Kommunikation', pp. 194–433.

Schmied-Kowarzik, Wolfdietrich: 'Marginalien zu einer dialektischen Grundlegung der Pädagogik', in: *Pädagogische Rundschau*, vol. 26, 1972, no. 12, pp. 853–86.

Skovsmose, Ole: 'Mathematical Education versus Critical Education', in: *Educational Studies in Mathematics*, vol. 16, 1985, pp. 337–54.

Svi Shapiro, H.: 'Habermas, O'Connor, and Wolfe, and the Crisis of the Welfare-Capitalist State: Conservative Politics and the Roots of Educational Policy in the 1980s', in: *Educational Theory*, vol. 33, 1983, no. 3–4, pp. 135–47.

Young, R. E.: 'Critical Teaching and Learning', in: *Educational Theory*, vol. 38, 1988, no. 1, pp. 47–59.

—— 'Moral Development, Ego Autonomy, and Questions of Practicality in the Critical Theory of Schooling', in: *Educational Theory*, vol. 38 (1988), no. 4, pp. 391–404.

Wulf, Christoph: 'Kritische Erziehungswissenschaft', in: ibid., *Theorien und Konzepte der Erziehungswissenschaft*. München: Juventa 1977, pp. 137–207.

II (e)   *Ethics/Moral Development*

Apel, Karl-Otto: 'Sprechakttheorie und Begründung ethischer Normen. J. R. Searles Versuch einer Ableitung des Sollens aus dem Sein im Lichte einer transzendentalen Sprachpragmatik', in: K. Lorenz (ed.), *Konstruktionen versus Positionen. Beiträge zur Diskussion um die konstruktive Wissenschaftstheorie.* Berlin and New York: W. de Gruyter, Part II: *Allgemeine Wissenschaftstheorie* 1978, pp. 37—106. On Habermas: pp. 65ff, 70—3; 98—103.

——: 'Grenzen der Diskursethik? Versuch einer Zwischenbalanz', in: *Zeitschrift für philosophische Forschung*, vol. 40, 1986, no. 1, pp. 3—31.

Benhabib, Seyla: 'Toward a Communicative Ethics and Autonomy', in: *Critique, Norm, and Utopia. A Study of the Foundations of Critical Theory.* New York: Columbia University Press 1986, pp. 279—353. (Here also on Habermas: 'The Critique of Functionalist Reason', pp. 224—78.)

Burger, Rudolf: 'Lob der Niedertracht — Probleme in der Universalethik von Habermas und Apel', in: *Leviathan. Zeitschrift für Sozialwissenschaft* (Berlin-W.), vol. 16, 1988, no. 4, pp. 443—56.

Constantineau, Philippe: 'L'Ethique par-delà la sémantique et la pragmatique', in: *Critique*, vol. 42, 1986, no. 475, pp. 1210—24.

Ferrara, Alessandro: 'A Critique of Habermas' "Diskursethik"', in: *Telos*, no. 64, 1985, summer, pp. 45—74.

Honneth, Axel: 'Diskursethik und implizites Gerechtigkeitskonzept. Eine Diskussionsbemerkung', in: Emil Angehrn and Georg Lohmann (eds), *Ethik und Marx. Moralkritik und normative Grundlagen der Marxschen Theorie.* Königstein/Ts.: Hain Verlag bei Athenäum 1986, pp. 268—74.

—— and Hans Joas: 'Moral evolution and domination of nature. Jürgen Habermas's theory of socio-cultural evolution', in: ibid., *Social Action and Human Nature.* Cambridge and New York: Cambridge University Press 1988, pp. 151—67

Hooft, Stan van: 'Habermas' Communicative Ethics', in: *Social Praxis* (Den Haag), vol. 4, 1976—7, no. 1—2, pp. 147—75.

Howard, Dick: 'Moral Development and Ego Identity: A Clarification', in: *Telos*, no. 27, 1976, spring, pp. 176—82.

Ingram, David: 'The Possibility of a Communication Ethic Reconsidered: Habermas, Gadamer, and Bourdieu on Discourse', in: *Man and World*, vol. 15, 1982, no. 2, pp. 149—61.

Kern, Lucian: 'Praktischer Diskurs und Vertragsmodell im entscheidungslogischen Vergleich', in: Lucian Kern, Hans-Peter Müller (eds), *Gerechtigkeit, Diskurs oder Markt? Die neuen Ansätze in der Vertragstheorie.* Opladen: Westdeutscher Verlag, 1986, pp. 83—95.

Kitschelt, Herbert: 'Moralisches Argumentieren und Sozialtheorie. Prozedurale Ethik bei John Rawls und Jürgen Habermas', in: *Archiv für Rechts- und Sozialphilosophie*, vol. 66, 1980, no. 3, pp. 391—429.

Klumpp, Eberhard: 'Mündigkeit als ethisches Prinzip?', in: *Zeitschrift für philosophische Forschung*, vol. 27, 1973, no. 2, pp. 222—36.

Mara, Gerald M.: 'After Virtue, Autonomy: Jürgen Habermas and Greek Political Theory', in: *Journal of Politics*, vol. 47, 1985, no. 4, pp. 1036—61.

Moon, J. Donald: 'Political Ethics and Critical Theory', in: Daniel R. Sabia, Jr. and

Jerald Wallulis (eds), *Changing Social Science. Critical Theory and other Critical Perspectives*. Albany, NY: State University of New York 1983, pp. 171–88.

Pieper, Annemarie: 'Das ethische Fundament des praktischen Diskurses', in: ibid., *Pragmatische und ethische Normenbegründung. Zum Defizit an ethischer Letztbegründung in zeitgenössischen Beiträgen zur Moralphilosophie.* Freiburg, München: K. Alber 1979, pp. 146–74.

Reid, Herbert G. and Ernest J. Yanarella: 'Critical Political Theory and Moral Development. On Kohlberg, Hampden-Turner and Habermas', in: *Theory and Society*, vol. 4, 1977, no. 4, pp. 505–41.

Saiedi, Nader: 'A Critique of Habermas' "Theory of Practical Rationality"', in: *Studies in Soviet Thought*, vol. 33 (1987), no. 3, pp. 251–65.

Smith, A. Anthony: 'Ethics and Politics in the Work of Jürgen Habermas', in: *Interpretation*, vol. 11, 1983, no. 3, pp. 333–51.

Thomassen, Niels: 'Habermas' Discourse Ethics', in: *Danish Yearbook of Philosophy*, vol. 24, 1987, pp. 77–96.

Torpey, John: 'Ethics and Critical Theory: From Horkheimer to Habermas', in: *Telos*, 1986, no. 69 fall, pp. 68–84.

Welch, Sharon D.: 'A Genealogy of the Logic of Deterrence: Habermas, Foucault and a Feminist Ethic of Risk', in: *Union Seminary Quarterly Review* (New York), 1987, no. 2, pp. 13–32.

Weisshaupt, Brigitte: 'Überlegungen zur Diskursethik von Jürgen Habermas', in: *Studia Philosophica* (Bern/Stuttgart), vol. 44, 1985, pp. 78–88.

White, Stephen K.: 'Habermas on the Foundation of Ethics and Political Theory', in: Daniel R. Sabia, Jr and Jerald Wallulis (eds), *Changing Social Science. Critical Theory and other Critical Perspectives*. Albany, NY: State University of New York 1983, pp. 157–70.

—— 'Habermas Communicative Ethics and the Development of Moral Consciousness', in: *Philosophy & Social Criticism*, vol. 10, 1984, no. 2, pp. 25–47.

Wiggins, Osborne P. and Michael Alan Schwartz: 'Techniques and Persons: Habermasian Reflections on Medical Ethics', in: *Human Studies*, vol. 9, 1986, no. 4, pp. 365–77.

Wimmer, Reiner: 'Habermas' und Apels Entwurf einer argumentativen Ethik', in: ibid., *Universalisierung in der Ethik. Analyse, Kritik und Rekonstruktion ethischer Rationalitätsansprüche.* Frankfurt am Main: Suhrkamp 1980, pp. 21–58.

II (f) *Hermeneutics/Gadamer*

Davey, Nicholas: 'Habermas's Contribution to Hermeneutic Theory', in: *Journal of the British Society for Phenemenology*, vol. 16, 1985, no. 2, pp. 109–31.

Depew, David J.: 'The Habermas-Gadamer Debate in Hegelian Perspective', in: *Philosophy & Social Criticism*, vol. 8, 1981, winter, pp. 425–46.

Gadamer, Hans-Georg: 'Rhetorik, Hermeneutik und Ideologiekritik. Metakritische Erörterungen zu "Wahrheit und Methode"', in: ibid., *Kleine Schriften*, Bd.1. Tübingen: JCB Mohr 1967, pp. 113–30. Also in: K.-O. Apel e.a., *Hermeneutik und Ideologiekritik.* Frankfurt am Main: Suhrkamp 1971, pp. 57–82 (Here also from Gadamer a Reply to Habermas, pp. 283–317). English: 'On

the Scope and Function of Hermeneutical Reflection', in: *Continuum* (Chicago), vol. 8, 1970, spring/summer, pp. 77–95.
—— 'Hermeneutics and Social Science', in: *Cultural Hermeneutics*, vol. 2, 1975, no. 4, pp. 307–30.
Giddens, Anthony: 'Hermeneutics and Critical Theory: Gadamer, Apel, Habermas', in: ibid., *New Rules of Sociological Method. A Positive Critique of Interpretative Sociologies.* London: Hutchinson 1976, pp. 54–70.
—— 'Habermas' Critique of Hermeneutics', in: ibid., *Studies in Social and Political Theory.* London: Hutchinson 1977, pp. 135–64.
Giurlanda, Paul: 'Habermas' Critique of Gadamer: Does it Stand Up?', in: *International Philosophical Quarterly*, vol. 27, 1987, no. 1, pp. 33–41.
How, Alan R.: 'Dialogue as Productive Limitation in Social Theory: The Habermas–Gadamer Debate', in: *Journal of the British Society for Phenomenology*, vol. 11, 1980, no. 2, pp. 131–43.
—— 'A Case of Creative Misreading: Habermas's Evaluation of Gadamer's Hermeneutics', in: *Journal of the British Society for Phenomenology*, vol. 16, 1985, no. 2, pp. 132–44.
Ingram, David: 'The Historical Genesis of the Gadamer–Habermas Controversy', in: *Auslegung. A Journal of Philosophy*, vol. 10, 1983, no. 1–2, pp. 86–151.
Jay, Martin: 'Should Intellectual History Take a Linguistic Turn? Reflections on the Habermas-Gadamer Debate', in: Dominick LaCapra and Steven L. Kaplan (eds), *Modern European Intellectuel History. Reappraisals and new perspectives.* Ithaca, NY and London: Cornell University Press 1982, pp. 86–110. Reprinted in: M. Jay, *Fin-de-siècle Socialism and other Essays.* New York and London: Routledge, Chapman and Hall 1988, pp. 17–36 (here also: 'Habermas and Modernism', pp. 123–36; 'Habermas and Postmodernism', pp.137–48).
Kamper, Dietmar: 'Hermeneutik – Theorie einer Praxis?', in: *Zeitschrift für allgemeine Wissenschaftstheorie*, vol. 5, 1974, no. 1, pp. 39–53.
Löser, Werner: 'Hermeneutik oder Kritik? Die Kontroverse zwischen H.-G. Gadamer und J. Habermas', in: *Stimmen der Zeit* (Freiburg/Br.), vol. 96, 1971, no. 188, pp. 50–9.
Mendelson, Jack: 'The Habermas-Gadamer Debate', in: *New German Critique*, no. 18, 1979, fall, pp. 44–73.
Misgeld, Dieter: 'Critical Theory and Hermeneutics: The Debate between Habermas and Gadamer', in: John O'Neill (ed.), *On Critical Theory.* New York: The Seabury Press 1976 and London: Heinemann 1977, pp. 164–83.
Piché, Claude: 'Entre la philosophie et la science: le reconstructionnisme herméneutique de J. Habermas', in: *Dialogue* (Canada), vol. 25, 1986, no. 1, pp. 119–42.
Ricoeur, Paul: 'Ethics and Culture. Habermas and Gadamer in Dialogue', in: *Philosophy Today*, vol. 2, 1973, no. 4, pp. 153–65.

II (g) *'Historikerstreit'*

Devant l'Histoire. Les documents de la controverse sur la singularité de l'extermination des juifs par le régime nazi. Paris: Ed. du Cerf 1988, 358 p.

Diner, Dan (ed.), *Ist der Nationalsozialismus Geschichte? Zu Historisierung und Historikerstreit.* Frankfurt am Main: Fischer Taschenbuch Verlag 1987, 309 p.

Erler/Müller/Rose/Schnabel/Ueberschär/Wette: *Geschichtswende? Entsorgungsversuche zur Deutschen Geschichte.* Freiburg i.Br.: Dreisam-Verlag 1987, 172 p.

Gerstenberger, Heide and Dorothea Schmidt (eds), *Normalität oder Normalisierung? Geschichtswerkstätten und Faschismusanalyse.* Münster: Westfälisches Dampfboot 1987, 222 p. (Here a.o.: Barbara Hahn and Peter Schöttler, 'Jürgen Habermas und das "ungetrübte Bewußtsein des Bruchs"', pp. 170−7).

Hennig, Eike: *Zum Historikerstreit. Was heißt und zu welchem Ende studiert man Faschismus.* Frankfurt am Main: Athenäum 1988, 229 p.

Hesse, Reinhard: 'Weder Revisionismus noch Entmündigung. Einige Anmerkungen zur neureren Diskussion um die deutsche Identität', in: *L' 80. Zeitschrift für Politik und Literatur,* no. 43, 1987, August, p. 55−63.

"Historikerstreit". *Die Dokumentation der Kontroverse um die Einzigartigkeit der nationalsozialistischen Judenvernichtung.* Texte von Rudolf Augstein [etc.]. München, Zürich: Piper 1987, 397 p.

Hoffmann, Hilmar (ed.), *Gegen den Versuch, Vergangenheit zu verbiegen. Eine Diskussion um politische Kultur in der Bundesrepublik aus Anlaß der Frankfurter Römergespräche 1986.* Frankfurt am Main: Athenäum Verlag 1987, 180 p.

Kühnl, Reinhard (ed.), *Streit ums Geschichtsbild. Die "Historiker Debatte". Darstellung, Dokumentation, Kritik.* Köln: Pahl-Rugenstein 1987, 330 p.

Pulzer, Peter: 'Germany: whose history?', in: *Times Literary Supplement,* 2−8 October 1987, pp. 1076; 1088.

Torpey, John: 'Introduction: Habermas and the Historians', in: *New German Critique,* no. 44, 1988, spring/summer, pp. 5−24.

Wehler, Hans-Ulrich: *Entsorgung der deutschen Vergangenheit? Ein polemischer Essay zum "Historikerstreit".* München: Verlag C. H. Beck 1988, 249 p. (here also: 'Die Gegenwehr. Die Kritik beginnt: Jürgen Habermas', pp. 79−87).

II (h)   *Knowledge and Human Interests*

Apel, Karl-Otto: 'Types of Social Science in the Light of Human Interests of Knowledge', in: *Social Research,* vol. 44, 1977, no. 3, pp. 425−70.

Artus, Helmut M.: 'Erkenntnis und Interesse', in, ibid., *Integrale Soziologie. Voraussetzungen und Grundzüge ihrer wissenschaftstheoretischen Einheit.* München: W. Fink 1979, pp. 137−55.

Barreau, Hervé: *Connaissance et intérêt. A propos des thèses de Jürgen Habermas.* Strassbourg: Université Louis Pasteur 1975, 14 p.

Böhler, Dietrich: 'Das Problem des "emanzipatorischen Interesses" und seiner gesellschaftlichen Wahrnemung', in: *Man and World,* vol. 3, 1970, no. 2, pp. 26−53.

Bubner, Rüdiger: 'Was ist Kritische Theorie?', in: *Philosophische Rundschau,* vol. 16, 1969, no. 3−4, pp. 213−49. Reprint in: K.-O Apel e.a., *Hermeneutik und Ideologiekritik.* Frankfurt am Main: Suhrkamp 1971, pp. 160−209. French: 'Qu'est-ce que la théorie critique', in: Archives de Philosophie, vol. 35, 1972, no. 3, pp. 381−421.

Overend, Tronn: 'Enquiry and Ideology: Habermas' Trichotomous Conception of Science', in: *Philosophy of the Social Sciences*, vol. 8, 1978, no. 1, pp. 1–13.

Ruddick, Sara: 'Habermas (J.), "Knowledge and Human Interests", in: *Canadian Journal of Philosophy* (Alberta), vol. 2, 1973, no. 4, pp. 545–69.

Wisman, Jon D.: 'Toward a Humanist Reconstruction of Economic Science', in: *Journal of Economic Issues*, vol. 13, 1979, no. 1, pp. 19–48.

II (i)   *Legitimation crisis*

De Simone, Antonio: 'Les potentialités de crise du capitalisme tardif', in: *Actuel Marx* (Paris), no. 3, 1988, pp. 130–43.

Fach, Wolfgang and Jürgen Habermas: 'Kontroverse über "Herrschaft und Legitimität"', in: *Soziale Welt*, vol. 26, 1975, no. 1, pp. 110–21. Cf.: Friedrich W. Stallberg, 'Legitimation und Diskurs. -Zur Habermas-Analyse Wolfgang Fachs', in: *Zeitschrift für Soziologie*, vol. 4, 1975, no. 1, pp. 96–8, and the reply from Fach: 'Anmerkungen zu Friedrich W. Stallbergs Habermas–Verteidigung', p. 99.

Ferry, Jean-Marc: 'Habermas et le modèle de la discussion', in: *Social Science Information/Information sur les sciences sociales*, vol. 25, 1986, no. 1, pp. 29–52.

Girndt, Helmut: 'Drei kritische Thesen zur Legitimationstheorie von Jürgen Habermas', in: *Politische Vierteljahresschrift*, vol. 17, 1976, Sonderheft no. 7, pp. 62–71. Here also from Eberhard Simons, 'Drei kritische Zusatz-Thesen zur Legitimationstheorie von Jürgen Habermas', pp. 72–5.

Held, David: 'Habermas' Theory of Crisis in Late Capitalism', in: *Radical Philosopher's Newsjournal*, vol. 6, 1976, pp. 1–19.

Hennis, Wilhelm: 'Legitimität. Zu einer Kategorie der bürgerlichen Gesellschaft', in: ibid., *Politik und praktische Philosophie. Schriften zur politischen Theorie*. Stuttgart: Klett-Cotta 1977, pp. 198–243.

Holton, R. J.: 'The Idea of Crisis in Modern Society', in: *The British Journal of Sociology*, vol. 38, 1987, no. 4, pp. 502–20.

Japp, Klaus Peter: *Krisentheorien und Konfliktpotentiale*. Frankfurt am Main and New York: Campus 1975, 139 p. On Habermas pp. 26ff. and: 'Krisentheorie des Legitimationssystems und Resümee', pp. 63–76.

Kopp, Manfred: 'Die normativ-praktische Herrschafts- und Legitimitätskonzeption: Jürgen Habermas', in: ibid. and H.-P. Müller, *Herrschaft und Legitimität in modernen Industriegesellschaften. Eine Untersuchung der Ansätze von Max Weber, Niklas Luhmann, Claus Offe, Jürgen Habermas*. München: tuduv–Verlagsgesellschaft 1980, pp. 167–218.

Löwenthal, Richard: 'Gesellschaftliche Transformation und demokratische Legitimität. Zu Jürgen Habermas' Analyse der Krisentendenzen im "Spätkapitalismus"', in: ibid., *Gesellschaftswandel und Kulturkrise. Zukunftsprobleme der westlichen Demokratien*. Frankfurt am Main: Fischer 1979, pp. 58–84. English: 'Social Transformation and Democratic Legitimacy', in: *Social Research*, vol. 43, 1975, no. 2, pp. 246–75.

Miller, James: 'Jürgen Habermas, Legitimation Crisis', in: *Telos*, no. 25, 1975, fall, pp. 210–20.

Pfeufer Kahn, Robbie: 'The Problem of Power in Habermas', in: *Human Studies*, vol. 11, 1988, no. 4, pp. 361–87.

Plant, Raymond, 'Jürgen Habermas and the Idea of Legitimation Crisis', in: *European Journal of Political Research*, vol. 10, 1982, no. 4, pp. 341–52.

Rasmussen, David M: 'Advanced Capitalism and Social Theory: Habermas on the Problem of Legitimation', in: *Cultural Hermeneutics*, vol. 3, 1976, no. 4, pp. 349–66.

Riedmüller, Barbara: 'Crisis as Crisis of Legitimation: A Critique of Jürgen Habermas's Concept of a Political Crisis Theory', in: *International Journal of Politics*, vol. 7, 1977, no. 2, pp. 83–117.

Sumner, Colin S.: 'Law, Legitimation and The Advanced Capitalist State: The Jurisprudence and Social Theory of Jürgen Habermas', in: David Sugarman (ed.), *Legality, Ideology and The State*. London and New York: Academic Press 1983, pp. 119–58.

Thome, Helmut: 'Legitimitätstheorien: Der normativ-kritische Ansatz von Jürgen Habermas', in: ibid., *Legitimitätstheorien und die Dynamik kollektiver Einstellungen. Probleme der Verknüpfung von Theorie und Empirie*. Opladen: Westdeutscher Verlag 1981, pp. 29–43.

Utz, Arthur F.: 'Legitimität und Regierbarkeit', in: *Archiv für Rechts- und Sozialphilosophie*, vol. 72, 1986, no. 4, pp. 523–30.

II (j) *Marx/Marxism*

Arnason, Jóhann P.: 'Marx und Habermas', in: Axel Honneth and Urs Jaeggi (eds), *Arbeit, Handlung, Normativität. Theorien des Historischen Materialismus* (2). Frankfurt am Main: Suhrkamp 1980, pp. 137–84.

Aronowitz, Stanley: 'Habermas: The Retreat from the Critique', in: ibid., *Science as Power. Discourse and Ideology in Modern Society*. Minneapolis, MN: University of Minnesota Press/Basingstoke, Hampshire: Macmillan Press 1988, pp. 146–68.

Besnier, Jean-Michel: 'Le marxisme au passé', in: *Revue de Métaphysique et de Morale*, vol. 85, 1980, no. 3, pp. 387–411.

Cerutti, Furio: 'Habermas and Marx', in: *Leviathan. Zeitschrift für Sozialwissenschaft*, vol. 11, 1983, no. 2, pp. 352–75.

Fleming, Marie: 'Habermas, Marx and the Question of Ethics', in: Axel Honneth, Albrecht Wellmer (eds), *Die Frankfurter Schule und die Folgen*. Berlin and New York: Walter de Gruyter 1986, pp. 139–50.

Flood, Tony: 'Jürgen Habermas's Critique of Marxism', in: *Science and Society* (New York), vol. 41, 1978, no. 4, pp. 448–64.

Jay, Martin: 'Jürgen Habermas and the Reconstruction of Marxist Holism', in: ibid, *Marxism and Totality. The Adventures of a Concept from Lukács to Habermas*. Berkeley: University of California Press and Cambridge: Polity Press, in association with Basil Blackwell, Oxford 1984, pp. 462–509.

Kerber, Harald: 'Gesellschaftstheorie als Erkenntniskritik? Zur Kritik der Marx–Rezeption durch Habermas', in: W. Kunstmann, E. Sander (eds), *"Kritische Theorie" zwischen Theologie und Evolutionstheorie. Beiträge zur Auseinandersetzung mit der "Frankfurter Schule"*. München: W. Fink 1981, pp. 124–213.

Kimmel, Bruce: 'Althusser and Habermas', in: *The Human Factor* (New York), vol. 13, 1975, no. 1, pp. 90–106.

Kogge, Peter: 'Habermas' Marx-Kritik und sein Verständnis des Marxschen Arbeitsbegriffs', in: ibid., *Der Marxsche Begriff vom "menschlichen Wesen". Seine Bedeutung für die Erschliessung von Perspektiven in der heutigen Pädagogik.* Frankfurt am Main: Haag + Herchen 1980, pp. 236–67.

Oetzel, Klaus-Dieter, 'Vernunft und Parteilichkeit. Zu Habermas' "Strategie einer Rekonstruktion des historischen Materialismus"', in: *Leviathan* (Berlin), vol. 5, 1977, no. 4, pp. 552–77.

Rockmore, Tom: 'Habermas and the Reconstruction of Historical Materialism', in: *The Journal of Value Inquiry* (The Hague), vol. 13, 1979, fall, pp. 195–206.

—— 'Bemerkungen zum Neo-Marxismus: Sartre und Habermas', in: *Zeitschrift für philosophische Forschung*, vol. 36, 1982, no. 2, pp. 234–51.

Roth, Volkbert M.: 'Mit Marx an Marx vorbei? Histomat 1 und Histomat 2. Diskussionsbeitrag zu Jürgen Habermas' "Thesen zur Rekonstruktion des Historischen Materialismus"', in: D. Henrich (ed.), *Ist systematische Philosophie möglich? Hegel-Studien*, vol. 17. Bonn: Bouvier 1977, pp. 583–93.

Sarrazin, Thilo, Frithjof Spreer and Manfred Tietzel: 'Krise und Planung in marxistischer Sicht: Das Beispiel Habermas', in: G. Lührs e.o. (eds), *Kritischer Rationalismus und Sozialdemokratie.* Berlin: Dietz 1975, pp. 213–43.

Sensat Jr, Julius: 'Recasting Marxism: Habermas's Proposals', in: Piotr Buczkowski and Andrzej Klawiter (eds), *Theories of Ideology and Ideology of Theories.* Amsterdam: Rodopi 1986, pp. 123–46.

Treptow, Elmar, 'Habermas' Stellung zu Marx', in: ibid., *Aspekte zu Epikur, Lukács, Habermas.* München: Uni-Druck 1978, pp. 103–13.

Zimmermann, Rolf: 'Das Problem einer politischen Theorie der Emanzipation bei Marx und Habermas und die Frage nach ihrer ethischen Fundierung', in: Emil Angehrn and Georg Lohmann (eds), *Ethik und Marx. Moralkritik und normative Grundlagen der Marxschen Theorie.* Königstein/Ts.: Hain bei Athenäum 1986, pp. 239–67.

II (k) *Marxistic Critique, Orthodox-*

Bauermann, Rolf and Hans-Jochen Rötscher: 'Zur Marxverfälschung der linksliberalen "Kritischen Theorie" der Frankfurter Schule', in: *Deutsche Zeitschrift für Philosophie*, vol. 19, 1971, no. 12, pp. 1440–59.

—— and —— '"Neuformulierung" von Kategorien des Historischen Materialismus', in: ibid., *Dialektik der Anpassung. Die Aussöhnung der "Kritischen Theorie" mit den imperialistischen Herrschaftsverhältnissen.* Frankfurt am Main: Verlag Marxistische Kritik 1972, pp. 27–42.

Beyer, Wilhelm Raimund: 'Der Begriff "Interaktion" -eine Sackgasse im Verwirklichungsprozeß der Philosophie', in: *Deutsche Zeitschrift für Philosophie*, vol. 25, 1977, no. 3, pp. 305–21.

Damus, Renate: 'Habermas und der "heimliche Positivismus" bei Marx', in: *Sozialistische Politik* (Berlin), vol. 1, 1969, no. 4, pp. 22–46.

Domin, G., H.-H. Lanfermann, R. Mocek and D. Pälike, 'Zur Wissenschaftskonzeption von Jürgen Habermas als Repräsentant der "Frankfurter Schule"', in:

ibid., *Bürgerliche Wissenschaftsauffassungen und ideologischer Klassenkampf.* Berlin: Akadamie-Verlag 1973, Part 2, pp. 136–43.

—— R. Mocek and D. Pälike: 'Zu den Wissenschaftsauffassungen der sogenannten kritischen Theorie', in: G. Domin e.o., *Bürgerliche Wissenschaftsauffassungen in der Krise.* Frankfurt am Main: Verlag Marxistische Blätter 1976, Part 1, pp. 72–146.

Hahn, Erich: 'Die theoretischen Grundlagen der Soziologie von Jürgen Habermas', in: *Deutsche Zeitschrift für Soziologie*, vol. 18, 1970, no. 8, pp. 915–30.

Heiseler, Johannes von: '"Kritische Theorie" und dialektischer Materialismus', in: *Internationale Dialog Zeitschrift* (Vienna), vol. 3, 1970, pp. 322–38.

Kofler, Leo: *Technologische Rationalität im Spätkapitalismus.* Frankfurt am Main: Makol 1971. On Habermas also pp. 12 ff. and pp. 135–54.

Rolshausen, Claus: 'Technik und Wissenschaft als Ideologie', in: *Sozialistische Politik* (Berlin), vol. 1, 1969, no. 4, pp. 47–64.

Steigerwald, Robert: 'Revision des historischen Materialismus: Jürgen Habermas', in: ibid., *Bürgerliche Philosophie und Revisionismus im imperialistischen Deutschland.* Frankfurt am Main: Verlag Marxistische Blätter 1980, pp. 243–61.

Wegener, Reinhard: 'Jürgen Habermas und die Kritik der "Kritik der politischen Ökonomie"', in: *Mehrwert* (Berlin), no. 10, 1976, pp. 3–68.

II (l) *Modernism − Postmodernism*

Benhabib, Seyla: 'Epistemologies of Postmodernism: A Rejoinder to Jean-François Lyotard', in: *New German Critique*, no. 33, 1984, fall, pp. 103–26.

Bové, Paul A.: 'The Function of the Literary Critic in the Postmodern World', in: Joseph A. Buttigieg (ed.), *Criticism without Boundaries. Directions and Cross-currents in Postmodern Critical Theory.* Notre Dame, IN: University of Notre Dame Press 1987, pp. 23–50.

Dumm, T. L.: 'The Trial of Postmodernism. The Politics of Postmodern Aesthetics −Habermas contra Foucault', in: *Political Theory*, vol. 16, 1988, no. 2, pp. 209–28.

Gasché, Rodolphe: 'Postmodernism and Rationality', in: *The Journal of Philosophy*, vol. 85, 1988, no. 10, pp. 525–38.

Giddens, Anthony: 'Modernism and Postmodernism', in: *New German Critique*, no. 22, 1981, winter, pp. 15–18.

Hoesterey, Ingeborg: 'Die Moderne am Ende? Zu den ästhetischen Positionen von Jürgen Habermas und Clement Greenberg', in: *Zeitschrift für Ästhetik und allgemeine Kunstwissenschaft* (Bonn), vol. 29, 1984, no. 1, pp. 19–32.

Kimmerle, Heinz: 'Ist Derridas Denken Ursprungsphilosophie? Zu Habermas' Deutung der philosophischen Postmoderne', in: Manfred Frank, Gérard Raulet and Willem van Reijen (eds), *Die Frage nach dem Subjekt.* Frankfurt am Main: Suhrkamp 1988, pp. 267–82.

Margolis, Joseph: 'Postscript on Modernism and Postmodernism, Both', in: *Theory, Culture & Society*, vol. 6, 1989, no. 1, pp. 5–30.

Müller, Ulrich: 'Hermeneutik als Modernitätskritik. Kritische Bemerkungen zur Postmodernismus-Debatte aus Anlaß zweier neuer Bücher', in: *Philosophisches Jahrbuch* (Freiburg/München), vol. 94, 1987, pp. 209–21.

Nagl, Ludwig: 'Zeigt die Habermassche Kommunikationstheorie einen "Ausweg aus der Subjektphilosophie"? Erwägungen zur Studie *Der philosophische Diskurs der Moderne*', in: Manfred Frank, Gérard Raulet and Willem van Reijen (eds), *Die Frage nach dem Subjekt*. Frankfurt am Main: Suhrkamp 1988, pp. 346–72.

Reijen, Willem van: 'Miss Marx, Terminals und Grands Récits oder, Kratzt Habermas, wo es nicht jückt?', in: Dietmar Kamper and Willem van Reijen (eds), *Die unvollendete Vernunft: Moderne versus Postmoderne*. Frankfurt am Main: Suhrkamp 1987, pp. 536–69.

Slaughter, Richard A.: 'Cultural reconstruction in the post-modern world', in: *Journal of Curriculum Studies*, vol. 21, 1989, no. 3, pp. 255–70.

Watson, Stephen: 'Jürgen Habermas and Jean-François Lyotard: Postmodernism and the Crisis of Rationality', in: *Philosophy & Social Criticism*, vol. 10, 1984, no. 2, pp. 1–24.

Wellbery, D. B.: 'Nietzsche – Art – Postmodernism – A Reply to Habermas, Jürgen', in: *Stanford Italian Review*, vol. 6, 1986, no. 1–2, pp. 77–104.

Welsch, Wolfgang: *Unsere postmoderne Moderne*. Weinheim: VCH, Acta Humaniora 1987, 344 p. (Here on Habermas, pp. 159–65 and 270 ff.)

Wolin, Richard: 'Modernism vs. Postmodernism', in: *Telos*, no. 62, 1984–5, winter, pp. 9–29.

II (m)   *Positivist Dispute/Social Science*

Adorno, Theodor W. (e.o.), *Der Positivismusstreit in der deutschen Soziologie*. Neuwied, Berlin: Luchterhand 1969. English: *The Positivist Dispute in German Sociology*. London: Heinemann 1976. French: *De Vienne à Francfort. La querelle allemande des sciences sociales*. Bruxelles: Ed. Complexe/Paris: Presses Universitaires de France 1979. This work contains the Discussion between Habermas and Hans Albert.

Albrecht, Johann: 'Scientific Discourse and Practical Dialogue', in: ibid., *Planning as Social Process. The Use of Critical Theory*. Frankfurt am Main, Bern and New York: Peter Lang 1985, pp. 53–84.

Alford, Fred C.: 'Is Jürgen Habermas' Reconstructive Science really Science?', in: *Theory and Society*, vol. 14, 1985, no. 3, pp. 321–40.

Apel, Karl-Otto: 'Wissenschaft als Emanzipation? Eine kritische Würdigung der Wissenschaftskonzeption der "Kritischen Theorie"', in: *Zeitschrift für allgemeine Wissenschaftstheorie*, vol. 1, 1970, pp. 173–95.

Baier, Horst: 'Soziologie und Geschichte. Überlegungen zur Kontroverse zwischen dialektischer und neupositivistischer Soziologie', in: *Archiv für Rechts- und Sozialphilosophie*, vol. 52, 1966, no. 1, pp. 67–91.

Bonß, Wolfgang: 'Kritische Theorie als empirische Wissenschaft. Zur Methodologie "postkonventioneller" Sozialforschung', in: *Soziale Welt*, vol. 34, 1983, no. 1, pp. 57–89.

Brand, Arie: 'Interests and the Growth of Knowledge. A Comparison of Weber, Popper and Habermas', in: *The Netherland's Journal of Sociology*, vol. 13, 1977, no. 1, pp. 1–20.

Eisele, Volker: 'Theory and Praxis: The View from Frankfurt', in: *Berkeley Journal of Sociology*, vol. 16, 1971, pp. 94–105.

Esser H., K. Klenovits and H. Zehnpfennig: *Wissenschaftstheorie*. Part 2: *Funktionsanalyse und hermeneutisch-dialektische Ansätze*. Stuttgart: B. G. Teubner 1977. On Habermas pp. 176–216.

Factor, Regis A. and Stephen P. Turner: 'The Critique of Positivist Social Science in Leo Strauss and Jürgen Habermas', in: *Sociological Analysis and Theory*, vol. 7, 1977, no. 3, pp. 185–206.

Franzen, Winfried: 'Die Geisteswissenschaften und die Praxis. Kritische Überlegungen zu einem Aspekt der wissenschaftstheoretischen Konzeption von Jürgen Habermas', in: *Studia Philosophica* (Basel), vol. 36, 1976, pp. 52–83.

Keuth, Herbert: 'Zum Positivismusstreit', in: ibid., *Wissenschaft und Werturteil. Zu Werturteilsdiskussion und Positivismusstreit*. Tübingen: J.C.B. Mohr (Paul Siebeck) 1989, pp. 93–190.

Komesaroff, Paul A.: 'Habermas and the Positivism Dispute; Science and Interests', in: ibid., *Objectivity, Science and Society. Interpreting Nature and Society in the Age of the Crisis of Science*. London and New York: Routledge & Kegan Paul 1986, pp. 76–92.

Misgeld, Dieter: 'Modernity and Social Science: Habermas and Rorty', in: *Philosophy & Social Criticism*, vol. 11, 1986, no. 3, pp. 355–70.

Münch, Richard: 'Realismus und transzendentale Erkenntniskritik. Zur Kontroverse zwischen Kritischem Rationalismus und Dialektik', in: *Zeitschrift fur allgemeine Wissenschaftstheorie*, vol. 4, 1973, no. 1, pp. 98–107.

Sabia Jr, Daniel R. and Jerald Wallulis, 'The Idea of a Critical Social Science', in: ibid. (eds), *Changing Social Science. Critical Theory and other Critical Perspectives*. Albany, NY: State University of New York 1983, pp. 3–30.

Schnädelbach, Herbert: 'Über den Realismus. Ein Nachtrag zum Positivismusstreit in der deutschen Soziologie', in: *Zeitschrift für allgemeine Wissenschaftstheorie*, vol. 3, 1972, no. 1, pp. 88–112.

Schulz, Walter: 'Der Gegensatz von kritischer und analytischer Theorie in der Soziologie. Der Positivismusstreit', in: ibid., *Philosophie in der veränderten Welt*. Pfüllingen: Neske 1972, pp. 158–76.

Simon-Schäfer, Roland: 'Analytische Wissenschaftstheorie und Dialektik', in: *Erkenntnis* (Dordrecht), vol. 11, 1977, no. 3, pp. 365–82.

Vogel, Steven: 'Habermas and Science', in: *Praxis International*, vol. 8, 1988, no. 3, pp. 329–49.

II (n)   *Psychoanalysis/Freud*

Alford, C. Fred: 'Habermas, Post-Freudian Psychoanalysis, and the End of Individual', in: *Theory, Culture & Society*, vol. 4, 1987, no. 1, pp. 3–29.

Flynn, Bernard Charles: 'Reading Habermas Reading Freud', in: *Human Studies*, vol. 8, 1985, no. 1, pp. 57–76.

Grünbaum, Adolf: 'Critique of Habermas's Philosophy of Psychoanalysis', in: ibid., *The Foundations of Psychoanalysis. A Philosophical Critique*. Berkeley, and London: University of California Press 1984, pp. 9–42.

—— 'Die Epistemologie der Psychoanalyse bei Habermas', in: ibid, *Psychoanalyse in wissenschaftstheoretischer Sicht. Zum Werk Sigmund Freuds und seiner Rezeption.* Konstanz: Universitätsverlag 1987, pp. 29–51.

Lorenzer, Alfred: *Über den Gegenstand der Psychoanalyse, oder: Sprache und Interaktion.* Frankfurt am Main: Suhrkamp 1973, 173 p. On Habermas: pp. 134 ff.

—— *Die Wahrheit der psychoanalytischen Erkenntnis. Ein historisch-materialistischer Entwurf.* Frankfurt am Main: Imago-Druck 1974, 319 p. On Habermas: pp. 60–80.

McIntosh, Donald: 'Habermas on Freud', in: *Social Research*, vol. 44, 1977, no. 3, pp. 562–98.

Nägele, Rainer: 'Freud, Habermas und die Dialektik der Aufklärung. Über reale und ideale Diskurse', in: *Der Wunderblock. Zeitschrift für Psychoanalyse*, vol. 9, 1982, pp. 35–60. English: 'Freud, Habermas and the Dialectic of Enlightenment: On Real and Ideal Discourses', in: *New German Critique*, no. 22, 1981, winter, pp. 41–62.

Nichols, Christopher: 'Science or Reflection: Habermas on Freud', in: *Philosophy of the Social Sciences*, vol. 2, 1972, no. 3, pp. 261–70.

Reimann, Bruno W.: 'Therapie und Diskurs. Zur Problematik von Analogie-schlüssen', in: *Soziale Welt*, vol. 26, 1975, no. 4, pp. 469–77.

II (o)   *Public Sphere*

Arndt, Hans-Joachim: 'Strukturwandel der Öffentlichkeit', in: *Der Staat* (Berlin), vol. 3, 1964, no. 3, pp. 335–45.

Hohendahl, Peter Uwe: 'Kritische Theorie, Öffentlichkeit und Kultur. Anmerkungen zu Jürgen Habermas und seinen Kritikern', in: *Basis. Jahrbuch für deutsche Gegenwartsliteratur*, vol. 8, 1978, pp. 60–90. English: 'Critical Theory, Public Sphere and Culture', in: *New German Critique*, no. 16, 1979, winter, pp. 89–118.

Keane, John: 'Elements of a Radical Theory of Public Life: From Tönnies to Habermas and Beyond', in: *Canadian Journal of Political and Social Theory*, vol. 6, 1982, no. 3, pp. 11–49 (I), and: vol. 8 (1984), no. 1–2, pp. 139–62 (II).

Kemp, R. and P. Cooke: 'Repoliticising the "Public Sphere": A Reconsideration of Habermas', in: *Social Praxis*, vol. 8, 1981, no. 3–4, pp. 125–42.

Milde, Ulf: '"Bürgerliche Öffentlichkeit" als Modell der Literaturentwicklung des 18. Jahrhunderts', in: G. Mattenklott, Kl. R. Scherpe (eds), *Westberliner Projekt: Grundkurs 18. Jahrhundert. Die Funktion der Literatur bei der Formierung der bürgerlichen Klasse Deutschlands im 18. Jahrhundert.* Kronberg/Ts.: Scriptor Verlag 1974; 2nd. revised edition in 1976, pp. 41–73.

Mutz, Reinhard: *Sicherheitspolitik und demokratische Öffentlichkeit in der BRD. Probleme der Analyse, Kritik und Kontrolle militärischer Macht.* München, Wien: R. Oldenbourg 1978. On Habermas: 'Über manipulative und kritische Publizität', pp. 72–8; 'Zum Rationalitätsgehalt kritischer Öffentlichkeit', pp. 83–8.

Nuissl, Ekkehard: 'Strukturwandel der Öffentlichkeit?', in: ibid.: *Massenmedien im System bürgerlicher Herrschaft.* Berlin: Volker Spiess 1975, pp. 19–29.

Oberreuter, Heinrich: 'Parlament und Öffentlichkeit', in: W. R. Langenbucher (ed.), *Politik und Kommunikation. Über die öffentliche Meinungsbildung.* München: Piper 1979, pp. 62−78.

Rodger, John J.: 'On the Degeneration of The Public Sphere', in: *Political Studies*, vol. 33, 1985, no. 2, pp. 203−17.

II (p)   *Student Protest*

Abendroth, Wolfgang: 'Bemerkungen zu den Differenzen zwischen den studentischen Oppositionen und Jürgen Habermas', in: *Marxistische Blätter*, vol. 6, 1968, no. 6, pp. 77−83.

Bauss, Gerhard: *Die Studentenbewegung der sechziger Jahre in der Bundesrepublik und Westberlin.* Köln: Pahl-Rugenstein 1977, 353 p. On Habermas: 'Der Kongreß von Hannover: "Hochschule und Demokratie"', pp. 61−4; 'Karl-Marx-Universität in Frankfurt/Main', pp. 266−70.

Grossner, Claus: *Verfall der Philosophie. Politik deutscher Philosophen.* Reinbek bei Hamburg: Christian Wegner 1971. Second Edition: München: Nymphenburger Verlag 1981 (contains *c.* 40 p. on Habermas).

Hornung, Klaus: 'Protestbewegung und Hochschulreform', in: *Der Staat*, vol. 10, 1971, no. 3, pp. 357−82.

Vossberg, Henning: 'Zur Kritik und Selbstkritik der antiautoritären Bewegung', in: ibid., *Studentenrevolte und Marxismus. Zur Marxrezeption in der Studentenbewegung auf Grundlage ihrer politischen Sozialisationsgeschichte.* München: Minerva 1979, pp. 273−319.

Wolff, Frank and Eberhard Windaus (eds): *Studentenbewegung 1967−69. Protokolle und Materialien.* Frankfurt am Main: Roter Stern 1977, 253 p.

II (q)   *Theology/Religion*

Brown, David: 'Doctrine of Salvation. The social context: Salvation: Marx to Habermas', in: ibid, *Continental Philosophy and Modern Theology. An Engagement.* Oxford and New York: Basil Blackwell 1987, pp. 139−50.

Dienst, Karl: 'Religionsunterricht − Interaktion − Gesellschaft. Zur Theorie der "Symbolischen Interaktion"', in: *Der Evangelische Erzieher*, vol. 23, 1971, no. 1, pp. 10−22.

Gottwald, Franz-Theo: 'Religion oder Diskurs? Zur Kritik der Habermasschen Religionsverständnisses', in: *Zeitschrift für Religions- und Geistesgeschichte* (Köln), vol. 37, 1985, no. 3, pp. 193−202.

Hammer, Felix: 'Wie atheistisch ist die Kritische Theorie?', in: *Internationale Dialog Zeitschrift*, vol. 6, 1973, pp. 325−32.

Höhn, Hans-Joachim: 'Glaube im Diskurs. Notizen zur diskursiven Verantwortung christlicher Glaubensvermittlung', in: *Theologie und Philosophie*, vol. 60, 1985, no. 2, pp. 213−38.

Kodalle, Klaus-M.: 'Versprachlichung des Sakralen? Zur religionsphilosophischen Auseinandersetzung mit Jürgen Habermas' "Theorie des kommunikativen Handelns"', in: *Allgemeine Zeitschrift für Philosophie*, vol. 12, 1987, no. 1, pp. 39−66.

McCann, Dennis P.: 'Habermas and the Theologians', in: *Religious Studies Review*, vol. 7, 1981, no. 1, pp. 14–21.

Mörth, Ingo: 'La sociologie de la religion comme théorie critique (l'Ecole de Francfort)', in: *Social Compass*, vol. 27, 1980, no. 1, pp. 27–50.

Pannenberg, Wolfhart: *Wissenschaftstheorie und Theologie.* Frankfurt am Main: Suhrkamp 1973, 454 p. Here: 'Soziologie als verstehende Handlungswissenschaft', pp. 82–105; 'Hermeneutik und Dialektik', pp. 185–206.

Rohrmoser, Günter: 'Habermas', in: K.-H. Weger (ed.), *Religionskritik von der Aufklärung bis zur Gegenwart. Autoren-Lexikon von Adorno bis Wittgenstein.* Freiburg: Herder 1979, pp. 132–6.

Rothberg, Donald Jay: 'Rationality and Religion in Habermas' recent Work: Some Remarks on the Relation between Critical Theory and the Phenomenology of Religion', in: *Philosophy & Social Criticism*, vol. 11, 1986, no. 3, pp. 221–43.

Siebert, Rudolf, 'Communication without Domination', in: G. Baum, A. Greeley (eds), *Communication in the Church.* New York: Seabury Press 1978, pp. 81–94.

Siebert, Rudolf J.: *From Critical Theory to Communicative Political Theology. Universal Solidarity.* New York, Bern, and Frankfurt am Main: Peter Lang 1989, 305 p.

Sölle, Dorothee, Jürgen Habermas e.o.: *Religionsgespräche. Zur gesellschaftlichen Rolle der Religion.* Darmstadt, Neuwied: Luchterhand 1975. Here: 'Legitimationsprobleme der Religion', pp. 9–30.

II (r) Work and Interaction

Agger, Ben: 'Work and Authority in Marcuse and Habermas', in: *Human Studies*, vol. 2, 1979, no. 3, pp. 191–208.

Eickelpasch, Rolf: 'Arbeit-Interaktion-Diskurs. Zur anthropologischen Begründung der Gesellschaftskritik bei Jürgen Habermas', in: *Zeitschrift für Soziologie*, vol. 5, 1976, no. 3, pp. 201–14.

Eyerman, Ron and David Shipway: 'Habermas on Work and Culture', in: *Theory and Society*, vol. 10, 1981, no. 4, pp. 547–66.

Feig, Gottfried: 'Der Dualismus von "Arbeit" und "Interaktion" in einer "kolonialisierten Praxis": Jürgen Habermas', in: ibid., *Wissenschafts- und Praxisorientierung. Eine Analyse und Konzeption für die Arbeitslehre.* Frankfurt am Main, Bern and New York: Peter Lang 1983, pp. 61–9.

Holtkamp, Rolf: 'Habermas: Arbeit als instrumentales Handeln', in: ibid., *Wissenschaftstheorie zwischen gesellschaftlicher Totalität und positiver Einzelwissenschaft.* Lollar: Achenbach 1977, pp. 58–65.

Honneth, Axel: 'Arbeit und instrumentales Handeln. -Kategoriale Probleme einer kritischen Gesellschaftstheorie', in: ibid. and Urs Jaeggi (eds), *Arbeit, Handlung, Normativität. Theorien des Historischen Materialismus* (2). Frankfurt am Main: Surhkamp 1980, pp. 185–233.

Keane, John: 'On Tools and Language: Habermas on Work and Interaction', in: *New German Critique*, no. 6, 1975, fall, pp. 82–100.

—— 'Work and Interaction', in: *Arena*, no. 38, 1975, pp. 51–68.

Krüger, Marlis: 'Notes on a Materialistic Theory of Interaction', in: *The Cornell*

Journal of Social Relations (Ithaca, NY), vol. 11, 1976, no. 1, pp. 97–104.

Ladmiral, Jean–René: 'Travail et interaction dans l'oeuvre de Jürgen Habermas', in: D. Tiffeneau (ed.), *La sémantique de l'action.* Paris: Ed. du Centre National de la Recherche Scientifique 1977, pp. 259–70.

Morrow, Raymond: 'Théorie critique et matéralisme historique: Jürgen Habermas', in: *Sociologie et Sociétés* (Montréal), vol. 14, 1982, no. 2, pp. 97–111.

Ottomeyer, Klaus: 'Kritik der Verhältnisse von Arbeit und Interaktion bei Jürgen Habermas', in: ibid., *Soziales Verhalten und Ökonomie im Kapitalismus.* Gießen: Focus 1976, pp. 19–42.

Winfield, Richard: 'The Dilemma of Labor', in: *Telos*, no. 24, 1975, summer, pp. 115–28.

Index